LE FONDAMENTE NOVE

Castello

QUESTA DOPIA LINEA DENOTA IL CIRCONDARIO DELL'ARSENALE

CANAL DELLE GALEAZZE

ARSENALE VECCHIO

NOVISSIMA GRANDE

ARSENALE NOVO

CASTEL OLIVOLO

CANAL DI CASTELLO

PUNTA DI QUINTAVALE

RIVA DELLI SCHIAVONI

SQUERI DA NAVE

PUNTA DI S. ANTONIO

Isola di
San Giorgio
Maggiore

SERENISSIMO PRENCIPE

Inside Venice

TOTO BERGAMO ROSSI

photographs by JEAN-FRANÇOIS JAUSSAUD

INSIDE VENICE

A PRIVATE VIEW OF THE CITY'S MOST BEAUTIFUL INTERIORS

Foreword by
DIANE VON FURSTENBERG and PETER MARINO

Introduction by
JAMES IVORY

RIZZOLI
NEW YORK

New York · Paris · London · Milan

THE DISTRICTS

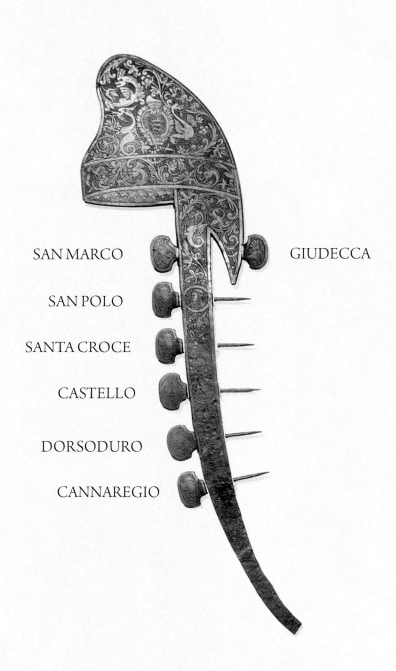

SAN MARCO

GIUDECCA

SAN POLO

SANTA CROCE

CASTELLO

DORSODURO

CANNAREGIO

CONTENTS

INSIDE VENICE

BY DIANE VON FURSTENBERG AND PETER MARINO

Venice, declared a World Heritage city by UNESCO, belongs not just to Italy but to the whole world. Beginning in the early Middle Ages, the Repubblica Serenissima entertained important trade and cultural relations with the known world of the time. It was the Venetian Marco Polo who reached the court of the Emperor of China, Kubla Khan, in 1271.

Venice's uniqueness made it something of a fourteenth-century Manhattan, which is to say an island where different cultures, nationalities, and religions came to coexist and interact profitably for centuries.

While in the other Italian and European cities palaces, mansions, and castles were fortified and inaccessible, in Venice the palazzi had loggias open onto the canals, and were faced with polychrome marble from Greece, Turkey, and Africa.

Venice was the most tolerant capital of Europe, ruled by a lay government, where already in the sixteenth century important international architecture competitions were held, such as that for the rebuilding of the Rialto Bridge, in which Michelangelo, Sansovino, and Palladio all took part.

The Serenissima held sway uninterruptedly for a good ten centuries, until 1797. The nineteenth century proved difficult for Venice, being marked by the foreign domination of France and Austria. The Serenissima was reduced from being the capital of an empire that stretched from the Dolomites to the Greek islands, to a mere province of the Kingdom of Lombardy-Veneto. Only in 1866 was it annexed to Italy itself but remained a relatively poor city until the 1950s, when the post-World War II economic boom exploded.

This long period of crisis did not facilitate the architectural development of the city in modern times, which, despite some localized projects, has reached our days very little changed from that depicted in the eighteenth century by the celebratory painter Canaletto and the more melancholy Francesco Guardi.

Toto Bergamo Rossi, better than anyone else, knows the artistic heritage of his native city. As director of the international organization Venetian Heritage, his efforts to save and to promote it are never-ending.

The author's intention with this volume is to illustrate the best of the Venetian decorative arts by his choice of select private residences, often inaccessible, as well as to give visibility to the public properties accessible to all. Bergamo Rossi has devoted a chapter to every *sestiere* or quarter, selecting certain masterpieces tucked away in museums, in churches, and in public buildings. Thanks to the sensitivity of photographer Jean-François Jaussaud, these are finally visible to all.

MY VENICE

BY JAMES IVORY

Where and how did I spend my very first night in Venice? Italy in the summer of 1950 was hosting the first Holy Year after the war, and the biggest wave of foreign tourists to arrive in the country since the beginning of the Second World War in 1939. I had come to Venice by train from Paris with no more than fifty dollars in my pocket, and had put up at a student hostel someone had told me about. This turned out to be a dormitory on the upper floor of a religious organization. The beds were steel army cots set up in rows in a big room with many windows, through which the clanging of church bells woke me at six a.m.—that sound is still perhaps my deepest memory of Italy. The bathing arrangements were primitive, and one was not expected to spend much time in this place during the day. You left your suitcase under the bed and hoped it wouldn't be rifled through while you were sightseeing. There was a curfew, and a lights-out. I turned in on the first of my two nights there exhausted, but happy to be at last in fabled Venice. I was awakened suddenly by an explosion of high spirits: a party of stark-naked, very pink young Scotsmen, like aliens from outer space, were whooping and leaping about over the beds where we lay, turning the sleepers onto the tiled floor, from which they sprang up ready to fight. These invaders had switched on all the lights and I can see and hear the scene to this day: a melée of muscular legs and bare prehensile feet, fists, balls, clan yells, and vomiting, until two harried-looking priests ran in clapping their hands for order, when the Scots at last finally fell down or passed out.

I took a train the next day, with only ten dollars left, but unharmed: a slim, serious young American with a high forehead,

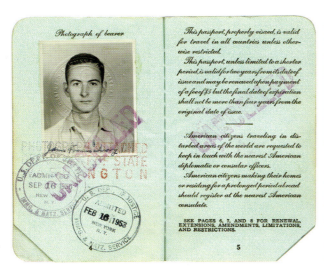

carrying his first of many, many passports safely buttoned inside his coat breast pocket, wearing a two-piece, grimy Brooks Brothers seersucker suit and a sweaty white shirt, whose ever-generous father in California had promised to wire him some more money, care of American Express, in Rome.

I would be back in Venice two years later to make my first film. In the meantime I needed to return to the University of Oregon for my final year at the School of Architecture and Allied Arts in order to obtain my degree. I was draft age, and liable for calling-up because of the American war in Korea that began in the same summer of 1950. I would be exempt from the draft, however, if I continued my schooling, so, after graduating from Oregon, I enrolled myself at the department of cinema at the University of Southern California in Los Angeles. I was aiming for a master of fine arts degree in cinema. In that two years I was away in Los Angeles however, I couldn't get Venice out of my mind. I had to go back, no matter what. I concocted the idea—seemingly

a novel one for my instructors in the USC cinema school—of making a film in lieu of writing a master's thesis. This was agreed to, and my father said he would fund it. I would write, photograph, and direct the film myself, though I had never operated a motion-picture camera before. I was full of that kind of enthusiasm a young man can often generate in himself and others when he has an idea, but which sometimes is not very well thought out.

I was proposing to tell the story of Venice through art. I was not an art historian, or a cameraman, but I was jumping right in to make a very ambitious film that professional filmmakers might have approached with more caution, after a lot of homework, and with an experienced team. Who was going to be on my team, my instructors asked? Why, I said, Gentile Bellini, Carpaccio, Veronese, Titian, Tintoretto, Canaletto, Tiepolo, Turner, Monet, and Whistler—what a roster of great names, of big stars!

Undaunted, I set out for Venice in the fall of 1952 with a new 16mm Bolex camera with three lenses, a light meter, and a tripod. What I could not carry myself, I was determined not to miss. I knew no one, and did not hire an Italian assistant, and could speak very little Italian. For practical as well as social reasons, that was a mistake. I have always thought of myself as someone other people have found easy to meet, to know, so my self-created solitude in Venice during the winter of 1952–53 seems strange and uncharacteristic now. People had always wanted to befriend me—that had happened in France, so why not in more convivial Italy? I could see that Venice was teeming with attractive people my own age who might be fun to know, as well as useful; why did no one come forward? I saw them from time to time, moving in groups through the narrow streets laughing and joking, even brushing against me.

I settled in at the Pensione Calcina, on the Zattere. A plaque by the door said John Ruskin had stayed there a century before, but I had not read him. The guests at the Calcina were better behaved than the naked Scotsmen; maybe too well-behaved. Conversation in the little dining room was a low, genteel hum, mostly in Italian. Some of the pensione residents had moved out of their grander quarters to save on heating bills. There was a very distinguished, slow-moving old lady in a long black dress which fell to the floor. She resembled, in her stateliness, the Dowager Queen Mary of England. She was accompanied by a younger companion, who spoke to her a bit too sharply sometimes, so that the rest of us looked up from our plates to glance discreetly. The food at the Calcina was a tasty and classical three courses of soup or pasta, meat or fish, and dessert—most often (too often) of a stewed fruit. But I was always ravenous after my exertions and ate up everything, including the tasteless white, hard rolls.

My dinners may have been lonely, but my days were full. If you have all Venice for subject matter and you own a good movie camera as I did, you quite quickly become a cameraman and develop your eye. I was out every day, in wind, rain, high tides in the Piazza San Marco, which you then had to cross on little, slapped-up, jiggly bridges. I was mostly happy, if alone, and sent off roll after roll of exposed film to my lab in Los Angeles. These contained images of what might be called Eternal Venice: the trembling reflections of marble church facades in the canals; the battle-ax prows of tethered gondolas bobbing up and down; Whistler-like distant views of the lagoons at dusk. Clichéd images for those who knew the city, but magical when you did not, like me.

Permissions were needed in order to shoot views of the Venetian medieval and Renaissance past seen in the mosaics of St. Mark's and the series of enormous paintings by Gentile Bellini and Vittore Carpaccio in the Accademia Gallery. How I went about that I no longer remember. Certainly I came prepared with a letter of introduction from the cinema department at USC, which must have gotten me in. Once admitted, I realized that I would need lights to photograph the paintings, the

dark surfaces of which absorbed all the daylight even on the brightest of days. These I was able to rent from the Scalera Studio, a defunct movie studio that had operated in Venice some years earlier. They provided me with six enormous lamps and furnished a pair of electricians to augment those of the Accademia. These lamps were terribly heavy, and stood on adjustable stands. They threw a very hot light on the pictures I was most eager to shoot, like the Saint Ursula cycle by Carpaccio. The museum *soprintendente*, Sig. Moschini, fretted that my lights would damage these very popular star pictures, and indeed they would have if placed too close or were kept on for too long. It is unimaginable today to subject ancient paintings like those to such stress. No picture gallery would allow it. But a lot was allowed at the Accademia. One day I was handed Giorgione's dreamlike little picture, *The Tempest*, to hold. It had been taken down off the wall for some reason while we were shooting. Everybody's hands being full, I took it. I remember studying it closely as I held it in my arms in its frame until someone was ready to hang it up again. I've read since that ephemerality and vulnerability are said to be the subject matter of *The Tempest*.

The *soprintendente*, a nervous man with good reason to be, paid periodic visits to us every day in order to reassure himself. His assistant however, a much less nervous man, Sig. Franceschini, organized things with the guard at the museum office next door to be telephoned on our set whenever the *soprintendente* was on his way. This was a half century before mobile phones. Then the lamps would be turned away from the picture we were working on in the direction of a stone-cold one. When the boss arrived, he would walk up and touch it and say, "Va bene." My co-conspirator, an unflappable, kind, and charming younger man, put in charge of the day-to-day matters of the shoot, was present at the horrifying moment when one of my top-heavy lamps began to rock, and then topple over into the middle of one of the big St. Ursula pictures. Before it could tear through the five-hundred-year-old canvas it was caught in the arms of the gang of electricians, a burning-hot, massive weight. This was a very sobering moment for all of us. If my lamp had continued its course, ripping through St. Ursula, I would have been expelled from Italy as "an enemy of art," and kind, openhearted Sig. Franceschini, my one true friend in Venice, would have lost his job. So, too, would have his boss, who would soon have discovered how mercilessly he had been tricked by us, and so ruined.

Winter nights on the Grand Canal: When I was not shooting in the Accademia, from where I could easily walk back to the Pensione Calcina with my equipment, and had set up in some other part of the city, I would take the vaporetto—or a motoscafo, which was more expensive for me—and return in stages to my quarters on the Zattere once it had gotten too dark to shoot. Most nights were very cold, but I didn't want to sit in the cabin, where everyone was smoking. I stood instead on the

 deck and looked into the brightly lit windows of the passing palazzi. Sometimes I saw into what seemed to be luxurious rooms: modern-looking drawing rooms with smart contemporary sofas and big lighted lamps, with shadowy, wonderfully painted beams above. As the weather was so cold, the big windows I looked up into were mostly shut, so I couldn't hear the owners' talk or laughter, or music from the radio, or from phonograph records (the first LPs had just come on the market everywhere), or hear any convivial sounds of ice clinking in highball glasses as you can in summer, or the popping of champagne corks—all sounds I supplied myself as I peered in. Sometimes I could see the lucky occupants moving about. I was the eager outsider with my nose pressed against the glass, looking in with longing eyes, as my vaporetto crisscrossed the Grand Canal from stop to stop.

I could not foresee that entire floors of some of these palaces I was passing—the best and most luxurious floors, the most beautifully painted ones—would someday be given to me to inhabit and throw parties in, in my persona to come of an esteemed foreign film director, one invited to the Venice Film Festival. Or that I could one day be standing on what was temporarily my own balcony, leaning there nonchalantly with my friends, glasses of champagne in our hands.

After spending all winter in Venice shooting my first film, while enduring an American presidential election there, when my beloved Adlai Stevenson was defeated by General Eisenhower, and the reaction to this in the Calcina dining room was a mere shrug, I went back to California. But during my last fortnight in Venice I finally became acquainted with a group of young Venetians, students like myself, who quickly became my friends. One night we all took a box at La Fenice to see *Il Crepuscolo degli Dei*—"The Twilight of the Gods." They alternated between necking on their gilded chairs and hooting in derision at the inadequate stage effects of Wagner's collapsing universe, but I liked them very much. They spoke acceptable English and I tried to make jokes in the Italian I'd learned. I was loathe to part from them so soon.

I would be coming one more time in my twenties, while on leave from the army in Germany in 1955, the draft having caught up with me at last. I shot more footage for my still-unfinished film, now called *Venice: Theme and Variations*. Then I vanished for eight years. I turned up in 1963 with my father and my partner, Ismail Merchant. We stayed at the Gritti Palace and had brought with us a print of our first feature film, *The Householder*, which we had made in India. We hoped to enter it in that year's Venice Film Festival, but the selection committee either didn't like it, or we had turned up too late, or both, and it was not chosen. My father asked to be shown the Pensione Calcina and I took him there, but everyone I'd known was gone.

After that I did not go back to Venice for more than twenty years, until 1986, having spent most of my life in India making films there. On this trip the rooms behind the closed windows on the Grand Canal opened up wide for me. I was coming in triumph with *A Room with a View*, soon to take on almost an Italian identity and to be renamed *Camera con vista*. Ismail rented a palazzo belonging to the ancient Marcello family, who had several of them, some on the Grand Canal, some not. Ours was in the San Marco area. At night I lay in a rococo bed, in what I recall was a pale green and gold room resembling the famous Venetian bedroom in the Metropolitan Museum taken from the Palazzo Sagredo, with my windows wide open to the summer nights. There was an extraordinary Muniments room, as they're called in English castles, containing centuries of records of the Marcello family: rolls of parchment with dangling seals, and great leather binders stamped with the years standing on shelves from floor to ceiling.

This was to be our custom when we were invited to the Venice festival, as it was at Cannes, when we happened to be going there, where we would rent a villa by the sea or in the hills. Ismail always filled up these grand establishments with our actors and cameramen and editors and writers, and also with our office employees from New York, London, and even Bombay—and when I say "filled" I mean "filled"—God knows where everybody slept. We all had to work. On your way to do press interviews you might be asked to come back via the market to pick up bags of rice because the numbers of journalists who had been asked to dinner had been miscalculated and Ismail knew he needed to throw together some Indian *keema*, dal and rice. One year at Venice, Ismail served on the festival jury but he somehow managed to entertain lavishly, giving orders to the cook in the morning before he left for the Lido in his speedboat. Those left behind had to fan out to search for a particular spice that would be needed, or go to buy more vodka for the press and the newly befriended celebrities that were expected. Somehow it all came together. This was Merchant Ivory's unvarying festival routine, and everybody liked it and looked forward to it. Five times at Venice: *A Room with a View* (Palazzo Marcello); *Maurice* (Palazzo Giustinian Brandolini); *Mr. and Mrs. Bridge* (Palazzo Albrizzi); *A Soldier's Daughter Never Cries* (Palazzo Dona delle Rose); and *Le Divorce* (Palazzo Mocenigo). And eight times at Cannes, but the names of all those French villas escape me now. Except for the Villa D'Andon at Grasse, which we took when we presented *Savages* at its world premiere in 1972 at the Directors' Fortnight. My comfortable room in the villa that night had been given to some grander guest by Ismail, and I returned when the festivities were over, in my tuxedo, to a cell I had been assigned to in a freezing turret, with a stone floor and a mattress of straw. But I didn't care, and fell asleep exhilarated by the fact that our first film at Cannes had been a resounding, sold-out *succès d'estime*.

Merchant Ivory's most recent visit to Venice was in 2003, when we came with *Le Divorce*, and virtually its entire cast, headed by Leslie Caron. Many of us stayed at the Palazzo Mocenigo at San Samuele. Like the Albrizzi palace, the Palazzo Mocenigo has a wonderful art deco bathroom, which was again my luck to draw. Those early 1930s, very elegant, twentieth-century bathrooms should be celebrated in their own right and possibly transported to the Metropolitan Museum too. Their designers (and their patrons) liked sumptuous combinations of red and black and silver, with many mirrors and generous numbers of light fixtures to make the whole place sparkle. There was a stupendous view from our balconies, right, left, and across—Ca' Foscari, Palazzo Balbi, another Palazzo Marcello, Palazzo Persico, the Palazzo Barbarigo—a study in style from the Gothic to the eighteenth century. Directly across was the San Toma stop of the vaporetto. How often I had gotten on there in the evenings after packing up, and looked across to the lighted windows of the twin Mocenigo palaces! Now I seemed to have come full circle and to have traded places with the starry-eyed young people in the passing boats, who perhaps may have come to Venice for the first time, and who, if they were looking up might have noticed a white-haired, elderly man silhouetted in front of an inviting room, leaning on the balustrade. He would be wearing, yet again, a Brooks Brothers seersucker jacket, in style as immutable, and unsusceptible to change, as the balcony itself. He would be looking up and down somewhat idly. Possibly his thoughts would be—as theirs might be too—full of gratitude at being in Venice, full of wonder.

The Stranded Gondola

In 2006 I made a film in Argentina based on the novel *The City of Your Final Destination*, by the American author Peter Cameron. It told the story of a rich German Jewish family named Gund, who emigrated to Uruguay in the mid-1930s. Among the possessions they brought with them was a real Venetian gondola—symbol of the lost European world they fled and a reminder of their honeymoon happiness in Venice.

When we shot our film we needed to have a genuine Venetian gondola; it was an essential prop. But there were none to be found in Argentina and surrounding countries, and, of course, no gondoliers. But we were able to buy, for five thousand dollars, a real Venetian gondola from its owner in Venice, and we found it on eBay. This lucky purchase must have been at the time when all the old gondolas in Venice were suddenly replaced by a fleet of new ones. Otherwise, what gondola owner would agree to sell the principal means of his livelihood? Our gondola was shipped to Buenos Aires and then brought up the La Plata River to where we were shooting; it was in good shape, and seaworthy you might say, and appears in the film as dictated by the story of the Gund family. But then a new problem arose: what to do with the gondola when we were done with it? I couldn't bear to abandon it in the South American jungle, so I had it shipped to my home in upstate New York, where it lives now. Unused alas, as there are still no gondoliers to propel it over my big pond at Claverack. Does anyone need a gondola? Who will give it a good home? I've offered it to Central Park in New York City, but they already have one, and a part-time gondolier.

About the time all this was happening with my gondola, I began to work on a new script. It was based on the Henry James novella *The Aspern Papers*, and our long-time screenwriter Ruth Prawer Jhabvala was writing it with me. Our plan was to update the original story first published in 1888 to the 1950s—to the time when I first went to Venice. It was to have been a full-length feature, and if it had been made, with certain adjustments necessary because of the updating, it would have been my only full-length dramatic film to be set in Venice.

On a visit there in 2010 I was shown the large garden James is said to have had in mind when he wrote his story, adjoining the Palazzo Gradenigo where Toto Bergamo Rossi, the author of this book, lives. In *The Aspern Papers* original story, an ambitious American biographer wheedles his way into the crumbling palace of the aged mistress of a long-dead poet like Lord Byron, in hopes of extracting letters the famous poet may have written to her half a century before (in our version he would have been someone akin to Ezra Pound). The American biographer energetically applies himself to the task of bringing the old lady's neglected garden back to life in the hope of ingratiating himself and earning her confidence; her drab spinster niece will fall in love with him. All his plans fail drastically, however (as mine did for the film, when I fell down some stairs and broke my leg). In time, the leg mended itself, but Ruth Prawer Jhabvala had by then stopped her work on the script and couldn't return to it.

Sometimes it's in the nature of planning a film that you end up after a lot of work with the ephemeral and the vulnerable—what the artist Giorgione's *The Tempest* is said to so beautifully embody—something to be dreamed of and pursued, into which you pour yourself for a time before you are forced by events to turn elsewhere.

James Ivory
New York, September 2015

SAN MARCO

Legend has it that in the year 826 some merchants of Venice made off with the body of St. Mark the Evangelist from the city of Alexandria, Egypt. The crafty Venetians decided to erect a basilica around the precious relic of the saint presumably found, who at the time, coincidentally or not, happened to be the only Evangelist without a real sanctuary dedicated to him in the Mediterranean area. The new basilica was inspired by that of the Twelve Apostles of Constantinople, then capital of the Eastern Roman Empire, and guiding light for the emerging Venetian oligarchy. The *sestiere*, or district, takes its name from the patron saint of the Serenissima, which also took for its own the symbol of the Evangelist, the omnipresent winged lion, with the book open under one paw, or closed if Venice was at war, and portrayed with paws between sea and land, which is to say between the Serenissima's dominions.

Until 1797 the basilica was called the Cappella Ducale. Only under rulers beyond the Alps in the nineteenth century was it turned into a patriarchal seat; as is widely known, right from the start the Veneto state confined the city's foremost ecclesiastical authority to the island of San Pietro di Castello. The Republic was a lay state. Still today the square celebrates the splendors of a glorious past, with the facade of the basilica acting as a backdrop to the huge space, faced with precious marble, featuring polychrome columns and decorated with bronze horses coming from Constantinople: all spoils of war that reached the lagoon following the conquest of the capital of the Eastern Empire in 1204. Venice is one of the rare Italian cities unable to boast a Roman origin. For that very reason it always tried to present itself as the new Rome. St. Mark's Square celebrates better than any other place in the city this perpetual quest for antiquity down through the centuries. A thick network of *calli* and *callette* branches off from the square, the widest of which affords quick access to Rialto, the city's ancient business district.

The bell tower, which once acted as a beacon for seafarers, keeps watch over the square and the city itself. The urban fabric of this neighborhood is tight-knit, with no broad open spaces other than St. Mark's Square and Campo Santo Stefano. Any land suitable for building has long since been used for this purpose. On either side of narrow canals are to be seen the fronts of numerous stately palazzi with precious sculpted details, almost in darkness, but present. The important thing was to be in what then was the metropolis of Europe. The concept of a home with a view had yet to be born.

Oddly, the island of San Giorgio Maggiore, site of a very old Benedictine abbey, also is part of the *sestiere* of San Marco.

PALAZZETTO ALVISI GAGGIA

The Gaggia home is formed by three buildings of different periods. The oldest, which dates from the first half of the seventeenth century, was built along classical lines by the patrician Giustinian family on properties previously belonging to the Michiel.

In 1876, the *palazzetto* became the Italian residence of Arthur and Katherine Bronson, well-to-do Americans keen on the fine arts.

Mrs. Bronson held a salon, where numerous guests and international travelers were received, including Henry James, her close friend, and the poet Robert Browning, who would stay at Ca' Rezzonico, the palazzo owned by his son, Pen.

In the 1920s, senator of the kingdom of Italy Achille Gaggia, who, with Vittorio Cini and Giuseppe Volpi, was one of the leading lights of Italy's economy and big industry of the early twentieth century, purchased Palazzetto Alvisi and commissioned famous architect Count Mantegazza to renovate and enlarge the building. By acquiring and then demolishing some minor buildings, he was able to create the splendid terrace on the level of the main floor and the side wing currently occupied by the combination salon and library. The important works carried out in those years, such as the staircase, the stucco decorations of the main floor interior, and the lovely flooring, coupled with the choice of the furnishings and objects still kept there, give this residence extreme elegance. The current owners, great-grandchildren of Senator Gaggia, still receive splendidly. The magnificent dining room, where a fabulous 1760 dinner service by Cozzi of Venice is displayed on one of the walls, is the setting for stimulating and elegant dinners with international guests with ties to the world of art and letters.

Everything is perfect in Chiari Gaggia's home, from the delicate lighting of the rooms to the excellent dishes served on eighteenth-century china. One always remains speechless looking out from the terrace opposite the Basilica della Salute, exactly in line with the main portal of the temple by Longhena, while to the left is to be seen the facade of San Giorgio Maggiore by Palladio, where at sunset the moon rises from behind the dome.

The room of the loggia is decorated in green marmorino *plaster.*
The furnishings and paintings date from the eighteenth century.
The table in the middle of the room is probably Russian, dating from
the onset of the nineteenth century.

The Room of Stuccos, so called owing to the ceiling embellished with
rococo decorations, also features Venetian furniture of the mid-
eighteenth century. The wall is adorned by a group of figurines by
Meissen, placed on small wooden shelves.

The library is furnished with mid-eighteenth century Venetian
furniture. Opposite: over a walnut console, four splendid views
of Venice, with original frames symmetrically decorating a wall.

In the dining room, a rare china service by the famous Venetian factory
of Geminiano Cozzi stands ready amid landscapes on canvas.
Above: a magnificent Venetian mirror of the first half
of the eighteenth century reflects the Basilica della Salute.

CA' FOSCOLO

Here we have a medieval building, renovated in the early sixteenth century, wedged between the stately buildings of Ca' Barbaro and Ca' Pisani. The palazzo's layout and facade follow the typical symmetrical tripartite design of most Venetian palazzi.

Detailed information about this building is lacking. It is known that for a long time it belonged to a branch of the old Foscolo family, who had important interests in Dalmatia and a lovely palazzo in Sibenik.

In the late nineteenth century, the palazzo became the Venice residence of the family di Serego Alighieri, who undertook a general redecoration of the second floor. Recently acquired by the current owners, it has been restored by architects Antonio Foscari and Barbara del Vicario, who reestablished the original dimensions of the rooms, retaining the traces of certain interventions that followed one another over the centuries, such as the late nineteenth-century floor of the salon, which contrasts with the Renaissance beams and with the new lime and *coccio pesto* (crushed earthenware) plastering. Some important Venetian paintings adorn the large walls.

CA' MOCENIGO NERO

The Mocenigo family, second only to the Contarinis, gave seven doges to the Serenissima. It was the only family that could boast ownership of four communicating palazzi on the Grand Canal. The first, called Casa Vecchia, was rebuilt in the seventeenth century and recalls the manner of Longhena. Another branch of the same family purchased from the Falier some properties adjacent to Casa Vecchia, and around 1570 built Casa Nova, with a facade imitative of a classical style completely built of Istrian stone. A few years later Casa Vecchia and Casa Nova were joined by the building of twin palazzi, the facades of which were decorated with frescoes by Benedetto Caliari.

While the construction of Casa Nova—also known as Mocenigo Nero, owing to the thick patina that accumulated on the facade over the centuries—has been attributed to the most celebrated architects of the latter half of the sixteenth century, such as Andrea Palladio, Guglielmo dei Grigi, Alessandro Vittoria, and Da Ponte, to date, the true identity of the author remains uncertain. The rooms contained a wealth of important art collections. Until a few years prior to World War II, the ceiling of one of them boasted a work by Gian Battista Tiepolo, depicting Aurora dispersing the clouds of night, and which is now housed at the Museum of Fine Arts, Boston. The famous coffered ceiling by Sebastiano Ricci is now installed at the Gemaldegalerie of Berlin.

The de Robilant family, heir to the Mocenigo di San Samuele, almost completely alienated the precious artistic heritage of the palazzi. Shipowner Arnaldo Bennati bought the palazzo shortly before the outbreak of World War II. An able businessman, he had the building completely restored, with the addition of a new wing and a garden with a ground entrance.

Master mosaic workers of Murano, active at the time at the Hotel Bauer, decorated some of the palazzo's rooms with typical art deco motifs. Part of the palazzo is still owned by shipowner Bennati's granddaughter, Francesca Bortolotto Possati.

Positioned on either side of a staircase spectacularly divided into two flights are two large wooden angel candleholders dating from the seventeenth century and two lanterns with three arms, which in bygone times adorned the sterns of the galleons of the Serenissima. Opposite: the sixteenth-century ground entrance of the palazzo, viewed from the garden.

The end of the portego of the palazzo is divided by a wooden wall and
leaded windowpanes, and echoes the design of the triple lancet window
of the counterfacade, called serliana. Opposite: a magnificent carved and
painted Venetian cradle dating from the early eighteenth century,
from the Donà dalle Rose collection, dispersed in the 1930s.

A HOUSE ON CAMPIELLO PISANI

Behind one of the stone arches spectacularly closing Campo Pisani is a less imposing house that forms a right angle on the square itself and affords a marvelous and unusual view of the stately facades of Ca' Pisani, now Conservatorio. The massive nearby palazzo, with its sculpted and overhanging details, is a looming presence from all windows of the apartment, again seen in the black-and-white photographs of its courtyards and rooms that decorate the living room walls.

Barbara Foscari del Vicario attended to the project down to the last detail, maintaining everywhere the two-color scheme for furnishings and walls, and wood for the flooring and preexistent wooden structures.

The great architectural mass of Palazzo Pisani seen from the windows and skylight. Over the sofa, designed by Barbara Foscari, is a photograph by Matthias Schaller of the main floor of a nearby palazzo.

GARDEN OF PALAZZO MALIPIERO BARNABÒ

Without a doubt, the Malipiero Barnabò garden is the most striking of Venice's gardens; it grandly overlooks the Grand Canal, between Campo San Samuele and Ca' del Duca.

The Soranzo family built the first cluster of houses in Veneto-Byzantine style. The property later was passed on to the Cappello family, of the branch known as del Banco, and was enlarged and elevated. At the end of the sixteenth century, the Malipieros, descendants of the doge Pasquale, rented part of the palazzo, and subsequently, through the marriage of a Malipiero to the heir of the Cappello family, came to own the whole building. In the next century the Malipieros further altered the palazzo by building the current baroque facade facing the Grand Canal. Between the two world wars, after the property had changed hands several times, the palazzo was purchased by the Barnabò family, who still owns it today. Famed art historian Nino Barbantini designed the garden and restored the main floor interior. Barbantini, a man of great taste and an expert in historical restorations, created a formal Italian garden and recommended the purchase of lovely garden statues fashioned from *pietra tenera* of Vicenza, eighteenth-century works by Antonio Bonazza. Acting as a backdrop to the austere entry hall is the architectural nymphaeum that houses the statue of Neptune, positioned on the garden wall. It seems that this architectural structure comes from the garden of Palazzo Cavazza, which later was destroyed in the nineteenth century to make room for the Santa Lucia train station. For more than thirty years, Anna Barnabò has diligently devoted herself to the care of the garden. Her efforts are rewarded with the fabulous blooming of myriad varieties of roses.

Low boxwood hedges geometrically describe the parterre of the garden and enclose roses and irises. Opposite: the entrance from the courtyard to the garden is adorned by two eighteenth-century sculptural groups depicting Ganymede and Jupiter (left) and Antaeus and Hercules (right).

HOTEL BAUER

A few years prior to the unification of Italy, Julius Grünwald cast his lot with that of a man named Bauer, whose daughter he wed shortly thereafter. Thus was born the felicitous Bauer-Grünwald hotel alliance, which enjoyed so much fortune in Venice and in Europe. A group of houses was purchased, and afterward demolished, which went from Campo San Moisè to the Grand Canal, where there were no buildings of particular importance. Architect Sardi—the same who, several years later, built the Hotel Excelsior on the Venice Lido—built the new hotel in a Gothic revival style. The hotel remained basically unchanged over the years. In 1930, shipowner Arnaldo Bennati of Liguria bought the hotel concern.

Impending World War II and the decision to modernize the hotel led to its closing from 1940 to 1949. The Gothic Revival facade on the Grand Canal was kept, while the new wing and the interior were completely renovated. When Hotel Bauer reopened for business, it was the most modern of Venice's hotels; its new modernist facade on Campo San Moisè took people aback and gave rise to criticism. These were the years of the postwar boom, and the international jet set began to regularly frequent the hotel. Those who stayed there include King Farouk, the royal family of Denmark, the Aga Khan, Ginger Rogers, Maria Callas, Arthur Rubinstein, Rudolph Nureyev, and many others.

In 1973 part of the famous cult movie Don't Look Now by
Nicolas Roeg, with Julie Christie and Donald Sutherland, was
shot at the Bauer. In 2012, Madonna stayed there on the occasion
of the presentation of her film W. E. at the Mostra del Cinema
of Venice. A major renovation project by Francesca Bortolotto
Possati, granddaughter of Arnaldo Bennati, has returned the hotel
to its former splendor.
The Hotel Bauer still has an important collection
of glass objects by Archimede Seguso, executed expressly
for the decoration of the hotel in the 1940s.

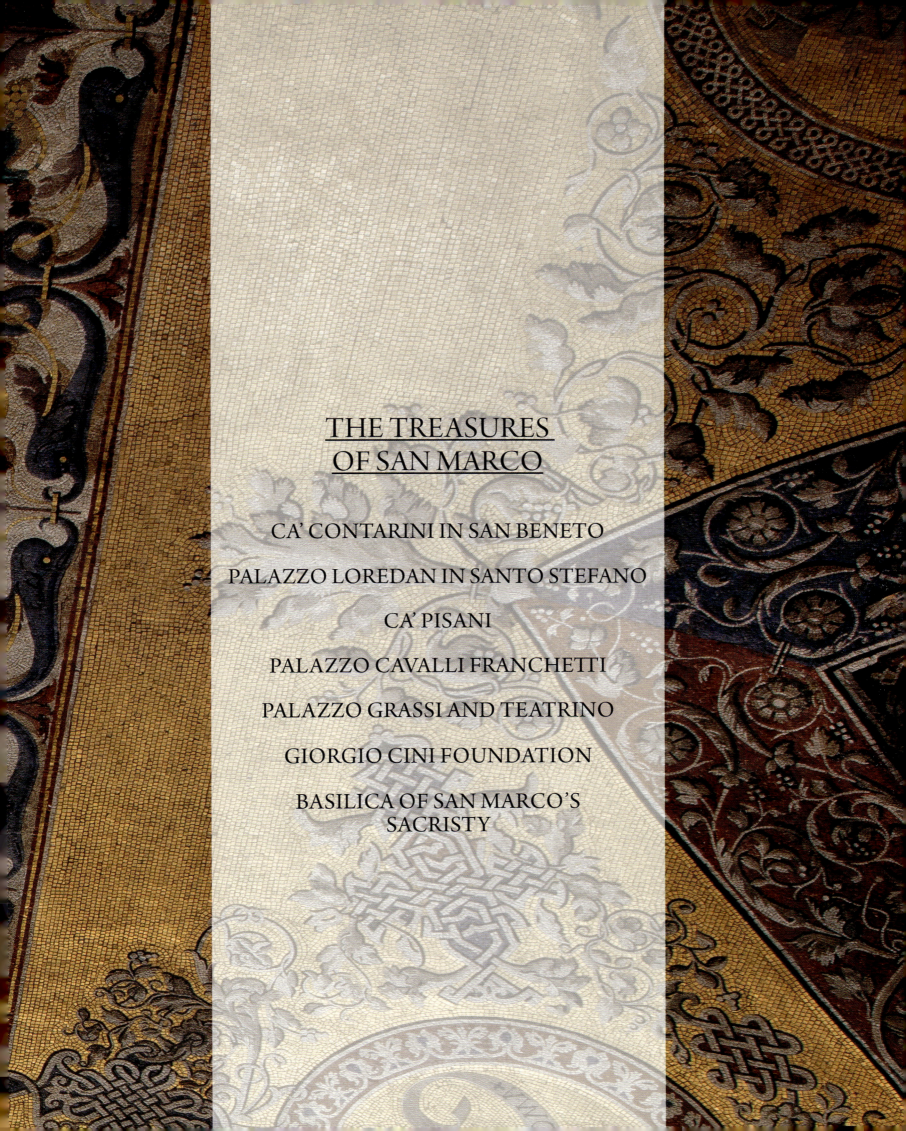

THE TREASURES OF SAN MARCO

CA' CONTARINI
IN SAN BENETO

The most generous genealogists trace back the origin of the Contarini to the Aurelia Cotta gens of Rome, which, once obtaining the Rhine prefecture, was called Cotta-Reni, or perhaps Conti del Reno, later becoming Contarini.

What is certain is that Marco Contarini was one of the twelve citizens to elect the first doge of the Serenissima in 697. This marked the beginning of the family being numbered among those known as "apostolic." The Contarini can boast of having given a record number of eight doges to the Serenissima. Over the centuries the family split off into eighteen distinct branches. The founder of the Contarini family of San Beneto, of the Ronzoneti branch, was a certain Beneto who lived in the early fifteenth century. His grandson was one of the most celebrated generals of the Serenissima, and the reconstruction of the palazzo in the present form can probably be attributed to his grandsons. In 1527 he obtained from Francis I of France a right to the fleur de lis that from then on the Contarini of this branch bore in a quarter section of their coat of arms. The architecture of the building is traditionally attributed to Sante Lombardo, son of the great Tullio.

The lovely facade on the small canal of San Luca is completely faced in Istrian stone with polychrome marble incrustations. In 1658, Domenico Contarini was elected the 114th doge of the Republic of Venice. The residence continued to be enriched with important artworks, maintaining nearly unaltered its sixteenth-century structure. In 1748 the palazzo was completely redecorated by the best artists of the period to celebrate the wedding of Giulio Contarini and Eleonora Morosini.

The main floor is perhaps the most complete example of a Venetian dwelling of the mid-eighteenth century. Everything is in Louis Quinze–style, from the fabulous Venetian terrazzo floors to the doors still with their original hardware, the stuccowork by Carpoforo Mazzetti Tencalla, and the frescoes by Fontebasso, Diziani, and Brusaferro. On the same occasion the "Casino di società" was built and connected to the palazzo by two raised passageways, its small rooms decorated with draperies and stucco parrots and oils in imitation of golden leathers. The last room of the enfilade of the Casino is decorated in Dutch style, with Delft wall and ceiling tiles framed by stucco friezes.

The palazzo was recently purchased by the municipal government, which a short time ago resolved to assign it to the Civic Museums Foundation of Venice as the future home of the Museo della Casa Veneziana (Museum of the Venetian House). The Venetian Heritage Foundation will coordinate the fundraising campaign for the restoration of the splendid interior.

The Ridotto, or Casino di società of Ca'
Contarini in San Beneto, built in 1748 in front
of the palazzo entrance, is joined to the same

by covered walkways on the main floor level.
Every room is decorated with elegant
polychrome stuccos.

The small wardrobe room is painted with
geometric and ornamental motifs.

The last room of the enfilade of the Ridotto is decorated unusually with valuable Delft tiles *applied to the walls and ceiling, and framed by stucco friezes.* *The small stucco shelves between the tiles probably held a collection of porcelain objects.*

The Venetian terrazzo floors of the palazzo, installed on the occasion of the Contarini-Morosini wedding of 1748, feature rich ornamentation and volutes, and are magnificently preserved. The finely sculpted fireplaces are often surmounted by large mirrors set in stucco decorations.
The ingeniousness of Carpoforo Mazzetti Tencalla was the driving force behind the conception and execution of the plastic decor of this sumptuous residence, where putti, cornices, racemes, flowers, ribbons, and volutes are exceptionally modeled.

PALAZZO LOREDAN IN SANTO STEFANO
VENETO INSTITUTE OF SCIENCE, LETTERS, AND ARTS

The old building, once owned by a branch of the Mocenigo family, was bought by the Loredan in 1536, who completely rebuilt it, assigning the work to Scarpagnino, then the most prominent architect of the Serenissima.

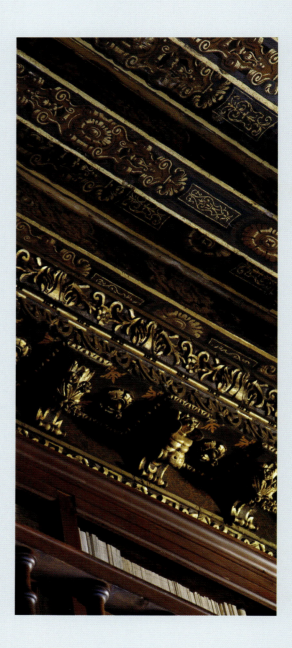

The facade along Campo Santo Stefano, rather free from architectural elements, was so conceived to be decorated with frescoes by Giuseppe Salviati and Giallo Fiorentino, which are today unfortunately lost.

In the entrance hall, which now houses an important collection of nineteenth-century marble busts, called the Veneto Pantheon, one can admire an imperial (double) Renaissance staircase.

In 1618 the front facade toward the campo was added; completely built of Istrian stone, it is the work of sculptor and architect Giovanni Girolamo Grapiglia, who had previously worked for the Loredan on the occasion of the execution of the monument dedicated to Doge Leonardo in the Basilica dei Santi Giovanni e Paolo.

Some of the main floor rooms are decorated with rococo stuccos, the work of Giuseppe Ferrari, and with frescoes by Giuseppe Angeli, pupil of Piazzetta, done in 1752 to celebrate the election of Francesco Loredan to doge of the Serenissima. This branch of the family, who provided the Republic with no less than three doges, died out in the late eighteenth century, upon which the important art collections began to find their way out of the palazzo, including the famous portrait of Doge Leonardo Loredan, a masterpiece by Bellini that for over a century now has been at the National Gallery of London. After the fall of the Serenissima, the palazzo became the seat of the first French governor of Venice, General d'Illiers. In that period, painter Giovanni Carlo Bevilacqua did frescoes on the mezzanine illustrating the deeds of Napoleon, which were plastered over during Austrian domination and recently discovered. After the annexation of Venice to the Kingdom of Italy, the palazzo became state property. Thanks to the testamentary legacy of Angelo Minich in the late nineteenth century, it was possible to carry out the first restoration work on the palazzo, and elegant furnishings were crafted for the library and reading rooms, which, starting from 1891, would become the seat of the Veneto Institute of Science, Letters, and Arts.

The sixteenth-century wood cornices of the palazzo are carved and decorated with gilding. The late-nineteenth-century bookcases hark back to the typology of archive furniture of eighteenth-century Venice, with the first order of cabinets surmounted by a gallery with balustrade and small rounded balusters.

Some of the palazzo's rooms are decorated with polychrome rococo stuccowork framing mirrors and forming medallions, within which are modeled vases decorated with small putti, horses, and garlands. The ceiling fresco (opposite) by Giuseppe Angeli, dating from the mid-eighteenth century, is framed by an elaborate stucco decoration that continues on the walls. The design of the Venetian terrazzo floor echoes the distribution of the stucco decorations on the ceiling.

CA' PISANI IN SANTO STEFANO
BENEDETTO MARCELLO CONSERVATORY OF MUSIC

The Pisani family made its fortune in remote times. From the fourteenth century on, it was known for its extremely vast mainland properties and for the profitable banking business in Rialto.

The Pisani split off into different branches and built some of the grandest palazzi in Venice. They gave numerous military men, cardinals, diplomats, and finally even a doge to the Serenissima. Alvise, elected doge in 1735, and his brother Almorò, were responsible for the realization of the villa, or better yet, the Pisani palace in Strà. The construction of the palazzo of Santo Stefano dates back to the first two decades of the seventeenth century. Then, the building had only one main floor. In 1728, architect Frigimelica was commissioned to add a second floor, and two new wings that would end in a ballroom twice the ordinary height, connecting them via open loggias. The palazzo's courtyards are real architectural "capriccios" that recall the pictorial inventions of Canaletto and Marco Ricci. A profusion of busts of Roman emperors and statues depicting virtues adorn the courtyards and entrance halls. The interior was sumptuously decorated by the most renowned artists of the period. Moreover, important inherited art collections found their way into the palazzo. The Pisani library was famous throughout Europe, and the picture gallery counted no less than 159 masterpieces, including works by Titan, Veronese, and Tintoretto. The descriptions of Venetian chroniclers about the festivities that took place in this residence in honor of the visit of King Gustav III of Sweden on May 5, 1784, are well known. But the end of the ancient Repubblica Serenissima had been long announced, and with its fall in 1797, and the consequent disastrous financial crisis, the fortunes of the Pisani also began to plummet. In 1807, Emperor Bonaparte purchased the Pisani villa in Strà for 973,000 gold francs. A few years later the famous library was sold, followed by paintings and various collections. Even the ceilings by Pellegrini that adorned the palazzo's library and ballroom were dismantled and sold. The former ended up at the Vanderbilts' Marble House in Newport, Rhode Island, while the latter decorates the vault of the Biltmore House in North Carolina. At the end of the nineteenth century, the palazzo was subdivided a number of times. The Venice city government then began to implement an enlightened policy of buying back the property, acquiring various apartments. In 1940 it was finally assigned to house the Conservatory of Music.

Previous page: a three-dimensional architectural whimsy, the magnificent loggia that divides the palazzo's courtyards.

The small oratory has an elegant eighteenth-century marble altar. Some monochromatic frescoes decorate the walls. Two rare doors inlaid with different types of woods—tortoiseshell and ivory—provide a further embellishment to one of the rooms on the upper main floor.

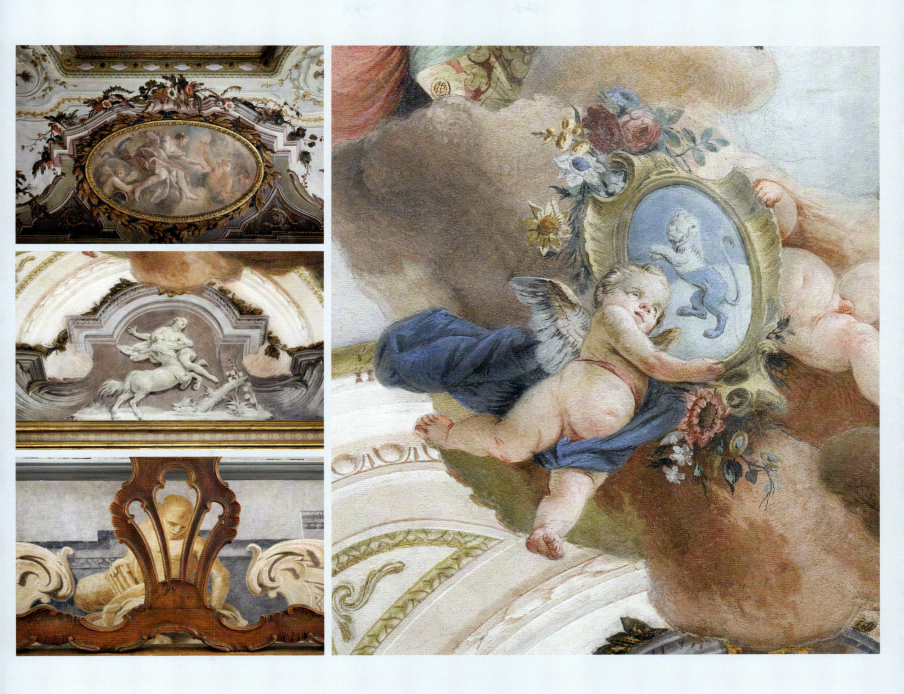

Most of the rooms of this surpassingly sumptuous dwelling are decorated with frescoes executed by Andrea Urbani, Jacopo Guarana, and Costantino Cedini, to whom we owe the two putti that bear the Pisani coat of arms.

PALAZZO CAVALLI FRANCHETTI
VENETO INSTITUTE OF SCIENCE, LETTERS, AND ARTS

The palazzo was built around the middle of the fifteenth century by the San Vidal branch of the Marcello family.
For more than three centuries, the Marcello, together with the Gussoni and the Cavalli, co-owned the building. During Austrian domination, Archduke Frederick of Hapsburg, Supreme Commander of the Imperial Navy, succeeded in merging the property, and undertook major restoration and modernization work.

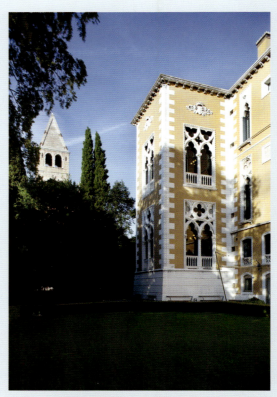

After the archduke's premature death in 1847, the palazzo was bought by Henry V, Count of Chambord, on behalf of the French legitimists. The new owner tasked Giambattista Meduna to carry out a series of major projects that resulted in the palazzo becoming one of the city's leading examples of Gothic Revival architecture. In those years, some minor buildings were demolished to make room for the new garden that still surrounds the palazzo.

In 1866, Venice was annexed to the Kingdom of Italy, and the Count of Chambord left the city on the lagoon forever. In 1878, Baron Raimondo Franchetti purchased the palazzo, and shortly thereafter assigned Camillo Boito—brother of Arrigo (Giuseppe Verdi's librettist) and author of the novel *Senso*—the job of enlarging and redecorating the whole building in Gothic Revival style.

Boito is responsible for Venice's most eclectic stairway, built between 1881 and 1884, faced with polychrome marbles and reliefs already reflecting art nouveau taste. In 1922, Baroness Sarah de Rothschild, Franchetti's widow, sold the property to the Istituto di Credito per il Risorgimento delle Venezie, which in turn sold it to the Veneto Institute of Science, Letters, and Arts in 1999.

Following extensive restoration work, the palazzo now hosts important exhibitions and meetings organized by the Veneto Institute, which has given life to a new cultural center among the most active in the city.

PALAZZO GRASSI AND TEATRINO
FRANÇOIS PINAULT FOUNDATION

The Grassi family, originally from Chioggia and elevated to patrician status in 1718, could boast four bishops.

After 1740 the wealthy family decided to entrust the construction of its new Venice residence to one of the city's most active eighteenth-century architects: Giorgio Massari, who was at the same time working on raising the third floor of Ca' Rezzonico, left unfinished by the Bon, on the other bank of the Grand Canal. The architecture of the elegant facade, imitative of a classical style and built entirely of Istrian stone, is a forerunner of neoclassicism. Nor does the plan of the palazzo follow the classic typology of the Venetian house: the building was designed like a Roman palazzo around a large central courtyard with a classic colonnade, and the *portego* runs along the facade. The monumental stairway, two stories high, was frescoed with scenes of society life by Michelangelo Morlaiter around the middle of the eighteenth century. It was the last grand private building to be built prior to the fall of the Republic. After the Grassi family died out in the first half of the nineteenth century, the palazzo changed hands several times, finally being purchased in 1857 by Greek banker Simone de Sina, who unfortunately altered the interior considerably. De Sina is responsible for the destruction of some eighteenth-century decorations, and closed off the double-height ceiling of the ballroom's portego, which was designed by Massari and frescoed by Canal. For a brief period it even became a hotel, complete with bathing establishment. At the beginning of the twentieth century, the palazzo was purchased by the Stucky family, who lived there until 1943. In 1951 it became seat of the Centro di Arti e del Costume, and many important exhibitions were organized there. In 1984 the FIAT Group bought the palazzo and continued to organize major shows until 2005, when French entrepreneur François Pinault decided to purchase the building to make it the headquarters of his foundation dedicated to contemporary art. The new owner assigned the renovation work to Japanese architect Tadao Ando, who, with the utmost respect for Massari's architecture, managed to adapt the palazzo's old volumes to new exhibition requirements.

Only very few Venetian palazzi were designed with two-flight stairways and a ceiling double the usual height.
Like a Roman house, the palazzo encloses the ample square courtyard. During the 1950s the monumental colonnaded open space was covered by a glass structure by Venini to house shows and other events. Already removed by Gae Aulenti in the 1980s, the structure was redesigned by Tadao Ando.
On the floor and walls is an installation by artist Rudolf Stingel.

In 1961 a small theater was built in an area behind the palazzo. In disuse since the late 1970s, it fell into a state of total disrepair. In 2013 once again Ando gave proof of his great planning ability: with just the 1,000 square meters of the theater area available, he realized an auditorium with a seating capacity of 225, and a real foyer divided by high curved walls.
A variety of cultural activities take place in the new facility, astutely promoted by the Pinault Foundation.

GIORGIO CINI FOUNDATION
SAN GIORGIO MAGGIORE ISLAND

Called "Isola dei Cipressi" for its cypresses in remote times, the isle was cultivated with vineyards and market gardens and had a mill owned by the Seigniory.

In 982, Doge Tribuno Memmo gifted it to monk Giovanni Morosini, who had the island further reclaimed and, around a small church consecrated to St. George, had a Benedictine monastery built, of which he was the first abbot.

In 1178, Doge Sebastiano Ziani made a significant bequest to the monastery and was buried there in the original church.

In 1223 an earthquake destroyed the entire complex. Doge Pietro Ziani promptly funded the reconstruction and, after abdicating, retired to the convent, where he died in 1229. Only at the beginning of the fifteenth century did the convent begin a real activity of studies and become a meeting place of scholars. In 1433, Cosimo I de' Medici sojourned there; in a token of gratitude, he had the convent's first library built. Designed by Michelozzo, it was unfortunately destroyed by a fire.

The dormitory, called Manica Lunga, is the oldest part of the convent. Designed by Giovanni Buora at the end of the fifteenth century, it stretches an extraordinary 128 meters in length. A Renaissance cloister was built, again on a plan by Buora. From 1559 to 1580, Andrea Palladio designed the refectory, the entrance cloister, and the monumental temple.

Baldassarre Longhena was assigned to build a stairway giving access to the abbatial apartments, and the construction of a library with a double order of carved wooden furnishings. After this unbroken string of magnificent projects, the whole complex went through very dark years.

In 1806 the convent was abolished, and its whole artistic heritage began to be dispersed, including even the famous canvas by Veronese depicting the *The Wedding Feast at Cana*, now at the Louvre.

In 1851 the complex was assigned to the Austrian artillery command. After a century of misuse, destruction, and neglect, the island rose again thanks to the institution of the Giorgio Cini Foundation, by will of Count Vittorio Cini and in memory of a son prematurely departed. The entire monumental complex was then restored.

At present it is one of the most famous institutions in the world dedicated to the promotion of the study of Veneto art and history, music, literature, and theater. Important international cultural events are held there.

Andrea Palladio designed the monumental cloister of the monastery of San Giorgio Maggiore, but did not manage to complete the work. A few decades later, Baldassarre Longhena conceived the imperial (double) stairway and the wing of the abbatial apartments that overlook the San Marco basin.

Recently inaugurated in the former Isola di San Giorgio boarding school was a new exhibition space called "Le Stanze del Vetro," for the glass objects displayed there. Involved is a cultural project born from the collaboration between the Giorgio Cini Foundation and Pentagram Stiftung, devoted to the study and enhancement of the art of twentieth-century and contemporary glassworking. Noteworthy among the important exhibitions organized are those devoted to Carlo Scarpa and to Napoleone Martinuzzi, and their collaboration with Venini. Thanks to the inexhaustible energy of Secretary General Pasquale Gagliardi, the foundation has recently been able to convert the Buora dormitory into an exceptional library. The project was attended to by architect Michele De Lucchi.

BASILICA OF SAN MARCO'S SACRISTY

In 1483, under the rule of
Doge Agostino Barbarigo,
a fire destroyed the old
sacristy of the basilica.

Three years later, the job of building what today is called the Sacrestia Nuova was assigned to the then proto of San Marco, architect Giorgio Spavento, pupil of Codussi. Spavento summoned Mantua carvers Antonio and Paolo Mola, members of a family of master carvers going back three generations, who had previously worked on the choir of the Certosa of Pavia and on the wooden furnishings of the Convent of Santi Giovanni e Paolo in Venice. Between 1498 and 1502 the Mola brothers crafted the wardrobes

of the sacristy, working from drawings probably by Vittore Carpaccio. In the upper portion there are twenty-one inlaid wooden panels—some of the Venice cityscape, others fanciful—which act as a perspective backdrop to scenes from the life of St. Mark. In some panels the contemporary architecture of the period was reproduced, such as the facade of the Church of San Zaccaria by Codussi, and the Church dei Miracoli, designed by Pietro Lombardo.

In the lower portion of the cabinets, the doors have a trompe l'oeil inlay, and behind the false open-work doors, which recall those of the Studiolo of Urbino, contemporary objects of everyday use can be seen. The ceiling is decorated with rare mosaics of the sixteenth century—no longer Byzantine, but rich in decorative elements of the early Renaissance.

*The sacristy of the Basilica of San Marco is ordinarily not open
to visitors since it is still used for its original purpose. But by
applying to the Procuratoria of San Marco, permission may
be granted to visit this fabulous place of the early Venetian
Renaissance, unknown to most people.
The inlaid wood panels depict, in false perspectives with early
Renaissance architecture, stories from the life of St. Mark.
On the opposite page is represented the martyrdom of the
Evangelist in a street of Alexandria, Egypt.*

RESTAU·MCMLXVII

SAN POLO

The quarter known as the Sestiere di San Polo takes its name from the church and surrounding square of the same name, which is second in size only to St. Mark's Square. The Church of San Polo was founded in 837. Rearranged a number of times down through the centuries, it still has its lovely Romanesque bell tower and flowery Gothic portal.

Some of Venice's famed festivities take place in Campo San Polo, such as the bull chase and other spectacular events. Venice's most characteristic area, and one of the oldest, is the Rialto, with its bridge and some surviving markets, the Church of San Giacometto dating back to the sixth century, and the huge Renaissance public administration buildings of the Serenissima.

During the Middle Ages, this was one of the most important trade centers in the world, where goods coming from Asia were dealt in, such as valuable fabrics, precious metals, and spices, as were foodstuffs coming from the mainland, islands, and sea. Ponte di Rialto links the Sestiere di San Polo to that of San Marco. The original bridge was built upon boats, called Ponte della Moneta because the old *zecca*, or mint, was located there, where the Serenissima minted coins: *zecchini*. In 1250 it was replaced by a wooden drawbridge to allow larger ships to navigate on the Grand Canal.

In 1497, Carpaccio immortalized the bridge in his famous *telero*, a large narrative canvas called *Miracle of the Croce*. The wooden bridge lined with shops on either side collapsed a number of times, so that in the early sixteenth century, talk began of building a new stone bridge. The greatest architects of the time were called on, including Sansovino, Palladio, and Michelangelo. The winner of the competition was Antonio da Ponte, who completed the work in 1591. Like the previous wooden bridge, the massive arch had shops on both sides, but this one was not planned with a drawbridge—a sign of the times; the maritime trade axis had shifted to the Atlantic after the discovery of America.

In 1514 a disastrous fire almost completely devastated the housing of the Rialto. Its reconstruction was assigned to Antonio Abbondi, known as Scarpagnino, who had recently completed the construction of nearby Fontego dei Tedeschi. Scarpagnino is also responsible for the reconstruction of the Church of San Giovanni Elemosinario, likewise collapsed due to a fire. The little-known church contains important works by Titian, Pordenone, and Palma il Giovane. In addition, Scarpagnino designed the Palazzo dei Dieci Savi alle Decime, one of the city's largest public buildings. Here is where the citizens of the Serenissima used to pay their *decima* (tax). In this quarter there are two Scuole Grandi—that of San Rocco, famous for Tintoretto's grand pictorial cycle, and that of San Giovanni Evangelista, with its stone chancel screen, executed by Pietro Lombardo in 1478.

The Basilica dei Frari stands out like a brick ocean liner amid the dense urban structure of the Sestiere di San Polo; along with paintings by Titian, Bellini, and the Vivarini, are the tombs of Canova, Monteverdi, and Titian himself. The Albrizzi, Barbarigo della Terrazza, Bernardo, Corner (designed by Sanmicheli), Muti-Baglioni, and Pisani Moretta Palazzi also stand tall amid the maze of very narrow streets of San Polo, locally known as *calli*.

PALAZZO BERNARDO

Built during the first half of the fifteenth century for the patrician Bernardo family, the palazzo had to be completed by 1442, when the Serenissima provided hospitality there to Francesco Sforza, Duke of Milan, and his wife, Bianca Visconti. The building has many architectural points in common with Ca' Foscari, the twin Palazzi Giustinian and Palazzo Pisani Moretta, and was probably built for two brothers, as often was the case in Venice, where primogeniture did not exist. Substantiating this supposition are two water doors and the completely independent ground entrances. The exterior Gothic stairs, built in two different courtyards, give access to the two main floors. In plain sight between the windows of the second main floor are the Bernardo coat of arms, sculpted within *aediculae* of early Renaissance taste. It is interesting to note that the two six-lancet windows of the second and third floor are asymmetrical, while all the other elements of the facade are symmetrical. The first main floor of the palazzo recently was restored by the current owners, who have reclaimed the original volumes with the utmost respect for the building. The magnificent *portego*, i.e., the connecting hall of Venetian residences, has been restored with the L-shaped layout typical of the Gothic period, and all the preexistent decorative elements have been saved and restored, with special attention to every detail: from the old wooden window casings and panes to the splendid Venetian *terrazzi* floors. Joseph Achkar and Michel Charrière, cosmopolitan experts in the restoration and decoration of historical residences, wisely advised the owners during the lengthy restoration process, and the result is truly exemplary, which is to say the best possible: one doesn't notice the new work. The dwelling is furnished with good furniture and paintings of different periods and origins.

The color of the plaster of this magnificently restored residence draws on the earth-base plaster that covers the facades of Palazzo Te in Mantua. The owners collect important Renaissance sculptures and seventeenth-century canvases by old masters.

Until a few years ago the main floor of Palazzo Bernardo was used
as university office space. Even the portego had been split up and the
original L-shaped layout that characterizes the salons of fifteenth-century
patrician dwellings was no longer visible. Thanks to the recent restoration
work, the original Gothic plan has returned.

The portego is illuminated by a set of old Dutch light fixtures.
The large canvases of "dinners" by Tintoretto tell us that the vast
salons of Venetian residences were lit by bronze or wooden
light fixtures. Murano chandeliers appeared only in the
eighteenth century.

*Precious velvet fabrics produced by the famed Bevilacqua
factory cover the high walls of the room used as a library,
on which hang some important paintings of the sixteenth
and seventeenth centuries.*

One wing of the residence is decorated with polychrome stuccos dating from the mid-eighteenth century. During the restoration of the alcove, an old pastellone floor the color of oxblood was found. The bathrooms are decorated with valuable bookmatched marble slabs.

CA' CORNER
ON THE RIO DI SAN POLO

The Corner family boasts remote origins. Some ambitious genealogists trace it back to the Cornelia gens of ancient Rome. For certain, present in the history of the Serenissima from the very beginning, it gave the republic numerous doges, procurators, cardinals, ambassadors, and even a queen—Caterina, married to the king of Cyprus and once widowed, gave the kingdom to the Serenissima and lived in gilded exile with her court in Asolo.

In the sixteenth century the Corner, divided into different branches, built some of the city's most monumental residences, such as Ca' Corner Spinelli, the work of Codussi; Ca' Corner, known as Ca' Granda, designed by Sansovino; and Ca' Corner on Campo San Polo, erected by Sanmicheli.

Little is known about the early history of Palazzo Corner on the Rio di San Polo, adjoining grand Palazzo Barbarigo della Terrazza, other than it dates back to the mid-sixteenth century and probably was unfinished. This theory is borne out by the singular facade overlooking the canal, which stops at just the first main floor with a cornice too plain to have been the final one. While unknown to us, the initial plan certainly must have been ambitious: the ground floor entrance hall is divided by four Istrian stone pillars that bear the large *portego* above, which is reached by a stairway adorned with polychrome marbles. The cubic shape, very high ceiling, and late sixteenth-century carved wood cornice of the *portego* recall certain rooms of Palazzo Ducale. The monumental archway on the main floor is similar to some portals designed by Longhena. Maestro Pier Luigi Pizzi, finding the palazzo in a ruinous state, had the bright idea of also making the entrance hall and former storerooms on the ground floor inhabitable. The effect is theatrical: from the all-white ground floor decorated with

plaster theater sculptures and bookcases everywhere, one ascends to the main floor, where the orange-red of the wall fabrics holds sway. The walls are hung with seventeenth-century paintings of the maestro's important collection, and Pizzi had furnished the residence with sumptuous furniture and old sculptures, as well as objects of his own design, such as obelisks and low tables.

The Ca' Corner dining room is furnished with two round tables.
Some important seventeenth-century paintings stand out on the walls.
The windows afford a view of the Romanesque bell tower
of the Church of San Polo.

The portego *is the setting of Maestro Pizzi's famed picture gallery*
featuring paintings of the seventeenth century. Architectural elements
and pedestals of his devising accent the ample space, acting as a base for
precious classical sculptures and Murano glass collectors' items.

Pier Luigi Pizzi has turned the monumental hall and adjoining rooms
on the ground floor into a study of architecture and stage design,
decorated with bookshelves, large plaster sculptures, tables, sofas,
a grand piano, and a famous work by Mario Schifano.

CA' GIUSTINIAN PERSICO

The palazzo overlooking the Grand Canal, directly opposite the four Mocenigo palazzi of San Samuele, was built for the Giustinian family at the beginning of the sixteenth century in early Renaissance style. Noteworthy are the elegant proportions and the finely sculpted details of the capitals and of the rosettes above the round arches of the windows. The large stretches of uniform red plaster with few architectural delimitations suggest the possible past presence of frescoed decorations, which probably were trompe l'oeil imitations of the precious polychrome marble incrustations typical of early Renaissance art. The Giustinians sold the palazzo to the Persico family in the second half of the seventeenth century. The Persicos, originally from Bergamo, were elevated to Venetian patrician status in 1685 for merits, military services, and especially the disbursement of no less than 100,000 ducats donated to the coffers of the Serenissima, at the time "distressed by the last Candia war" fought over the island of Crete, for years a bone of contention giving rise to wars between the Ottoman Empire and the Republic of Venice. The upper main floor of the palazzo has recently been restored by the current owners, who had the farsightedness to bring back the residence to its former splendor, rediscovering the elegant stuccowork and neoclassical frescoes that decorate some of the palazzo's rooms and arranging their impressive collection of contemporary art on walls of rooms flooded with light and the reflection of the water of the Grand Canal. The contrast is powerful and elegant, and the works fit in harmoniously with the historical context.

Giuseppe Borsato, architect, decorator, and painter in the service of the French Imperial court in Venice, conceived this magnificent neoclassical camerino (antechamber) decorated with grotesques and a frieze.

Opposite: a tapestry by William Kentridge adorns a wall of the portego. Art deco furnishings predominate. The Grand Canal can be seen from the quadruple lancet window.

On the dining room wall is
a work by Giuseppe Pennone. A neoclassical fresco
decorates the ceiling. Contemporary artworks are distributed
throughout the residence.

The drawing room decor is also mainly art deco.
The fireplace is of black Portoro marble with gold veins.
Some artistic installations decorate the walls. The Scarlatti light fixture
model was produced in 1924 by the famed Venini kiln.

PALAZZO COCCINA TIEPOLO PAPADOPOLI
AMAN RESORT HOTEL

In the sixteenth century the Coccina family, of Bergamo descent, became part of the Venetian nobility and tasked architect Gian Giacomo di Grigi to build a grand residence on the Grand Canal, with a facade in the classical style completely faced with Istrian stone. The palazzo was passed on to the patrician Tiepolo family, who had some rooms on the upper main floor decorated. During the second half of the nineteenth century, the palazzo became the property of the Counts Papadopoli, a wealthy family of Greek origin who settled in Venice at the end of the eighteenth century. They assigned the renovation of the palazzo to architect Girolamo Levi, who, inspired by Palazzo Vendramin Calergi, added a new wing to the preexistent building, and two gardens, one of which goes all the way to the bank of the Grand Canal. The interior decoration was assigned with no limit on spending to antique dealer and decorator Michelangelo Guggenheim, who embellished the salons with stuccos, gilded carvings, paintings, and large mirrors in line with Second Empire taste, interpreting early eighteenth-century Venetian style in a French Beaux Arts manner, then all the rage in Europe. It was the first Venice palazzo to be provided with an elevator, an intercom, and gaslights. The result bears witness to the taste of the age and the triumph of fin de siècle decorative arts. The upper main floor was only partially affected by the work done by the Papadopolis. One room is still covered with valuable Cordova leather, probably dating from the seventeenth century. In the same room is found a magnificent walnut burl bookcase-archive of the early years of the eighteenth century. Of particular value are two small rooms: a bedroom with an alcove, and its anteroom, the former decorated with voluminous stuccos that frame delightful frescoes by melancholy Giandomenico Tiepolo; the latter completely painted with chinoiseries and fanciful landscapes. The building was recently restored by Aman Resort and partially converted for use as a hotel. The palazzo is still the property of the Papadopoli heirs.

The ceiling of one of the rooms on the upper main floor of Palazzo Papadopoli is decorated with a fresco by Giandomenico Tiepolo. Over the lovely eighteenth-century fireplace, a large rococo mirror occupies the whole wall between the two windows looking out on the Grand Canal. The doors of the palazzo are embellished with bronze handles.

In a room on the upper main floor is a magnificent eighteenth-century walnut burl bookcase. The walls are covered with precious Cordova leathers, engraved and embossed.

The portego *on the same floor was not affected by the nineteenth-century redecoration. Neutral walls reflect the light.*

CA' ALBRIZZI

In the sixteenth century the Albrizzi family, originally from Bergamo, settled in Venice, where they became enormously rich, thanks to the trade of canvases and olive oil coming from Crete. In 1667 the Albrizzi also paid 100,000 ducats to the Serenissima to gain membership on the Maggior Consiglio. In the same century, they bought the sixteenth-century palazzo of the Bonomo in San Cassiano and wed their way into the leading patrician families of Venice. The main floor of the palazzo, famed for its white-and-gold high-relief stuccos by Abbondio Stazio, sumptuous furnishings, and important paintings, today still exemplifies the perfectly preserved Venetian patrician dwelling.

At the beginning of the eighteenth century the Albrizzi added a wing to the sixteenth-century palazzo, providing the main floor with an enfilade of rooms, and a ballroom decorated with the famed stucco cherubs in full relief, which hold up—or better yet, stud—a huge drape in the style of Bernini.

Around 1770, a large number of minor buildings were purchased and then demolished to make room for the ground level facade of the palazzo, thus forming Campiello Albrizzi. In 1820 the Albrizzi purchased the area previously occupied by the San Cassiano Theatre, and shortly thereafter, architect Meduna designed a romantic garden there, linking it to the palazzo by a small Gothic revival tower and a little bridge.

In 1983, mindful of the spirit of his forebears—who for centuries were committed to beautifying and renovating the palazzo—composer and writer Ernesto Rubin de Cervin Albrizzi decided to turn the attic of the palazzo into a fabulous apartment. And so the original sixteenth-century wooden trusses were restored, and in the central room, a bookcase in the style of Scarpa, designed by Ferruccio Franzoia, was installed to keep the rare books and the archive of the Zenobio family, who came to an end as such by marriage to the Albrizzi.

Preceding pages: The floor of the ample central space was conceived as
a labyrinth designed with pietra tenera Vicenza stone inlays of different
colors. Architect Antonio Foscari planned and directed the work.
It was his idea to keep and restore the old wooden stairs to the attic.

The terraces afford a magnificent view of the whole city and the lagoon.
After more than thirty years, the restoration work has not dated,
maintaining its elegant contemporaneity.
The sculpture is of Istrian stone.

THE TREASURES OF SAN POLO

CASINO ZANE

ARCHIVIO DI STATO

CHIESA DI SAN CASSIAN

SCUOLA GRANDE DI SAN ROCCO

CASINO ZANE
BRU ZANE FOUNDATION

Not far from Campo San Stin and the Basilica dei Frari stands Casino Zane, built between 1695 and 1697, and for a century, the place of entertaining at Palazzo Zane located just a few steps away.

The main palazzo—today the Livio Sanudo School—and the casino were separated by an elaborate French-style garden with geometric borders and statues. Unfortunately, the garden became a building lot in the early twentieth century, with only the well-known 1703 engraving by Carlevaris as a reminder of its past. The building adjacent the casino originally housed the famed Zane library, no longer in existence today. In 1682 the Baldassarre Longhenas' concern completed the renovation of Palazzo Zane as desired by Domenico Zane, who passed away in 1672 before the work was done, leaving his worldly goods—including a very important collection of books and paintings—to nephew Marino Zane. Marino was responsible for the construction of the casino and library, being desirous of preserving his uncle's collections, which he also had pledged to enrich. Architect Antonio Gaspari, with the Longhenas' concern, was charged with designing the casino; his assistant, Domenico Rossi, completed the work. The most important artists of the period collaborated to produce the extremely rich interior decoration. The voluminous stuccos are traditionally attributed to famed Abbondio Stazio from Ticino, while the hall's wooden balustrade, unfortunately stripped of paint in past times, is probably the work of the prince of Venetian carvers, Andrea Brustolon. Some frescoes have recently been attributed to Sebastiano Ricci. In 2007 the Bru Foundation undertook major preservative restoration that took four years to finish. Thanks to this enlightened project, the casino has regained the spirit of the period and is once again a place devoted to music and art, as originally intended.

Casino Zane, unlike some other ridotti in the city, occupies a whole building, originally built as a music hall. The recent restoration work has brought back to light some early eighteenth-century frescoes depicting architectural caprices and fanciful views. The stairway is decorated with frescoes recently attributed to Sebastiano Ricci and his school.

A small garden, adorned by Vicenza stone statues, serves as a ground-level entrance to the casino.

The door is embellished with typical Venetian windowpanes sealed with lead, while the windows on either side have

wrought-iron grates dating from the eighteenth century.

The decorative stuccowork of the music hall is the work of celebrated maestro Abbondio Stazio from Ticino, while the frescoes have been attributed to Sebastiano Ricci. The elegant balustrade, carved from a conifer known as cirmolo, was probably painted to imitate the stone and stucco. The concerts for the guests of the Zane family were performed from the balustrade.

ARCHIVIO DI STATO
FORMER FRANCISCAN CONVENT

Tradition has it that St. Francis himself founded the convent and the first Basilica dei Frari on lands owned by the Badoer family, then planted with market gardens and vineyards.

Over the centuries, the convent/complex underwent various transformations and enlargements. The two monumental cloisters bear witness to the importance of the role of the Franciscans in the city. The first, built in the sixteenth century, is enclosed by an arcade with round arches and surmounted by a terrace embellished with an imposing balustrade, on which stand some statues of Franciscan saints. In the middle is the most monumental well of Venice, conceived and sculpted by Francesco Cabianca, inspired by the well of the Zecca by Sansovino, now in the courtyard of Ca' Pesaro. The well-curb is flanked by rusticated twin pillars supporting an imposing stone lintel surmounted by an elaborate sculptural group depicting the Glory of the Trinity. Next to it is the cloister dedicated to St. Anthony, also built in the sixteenth century. The old fifteenth-century refectory, with magnificent columns that hold up ample cross vaults, now is used as a reading room of the Archivio di Stato (Public Records Office).

The Napoleonic decree of 1810 abolished the Franciscan order in Venice, and thus, the monumental rooms of the convent came to house the huge patrimony of Venetian records. The Public Records Office contains 70 kilometers of shelves with documents pertaining to the whole history of the Republic of Venice from start to finish, including documentary evidence of contacts with the world with which the Serenissima entertained political and economic relations and cultural exchanges. Few are aware that the system of embassies originated in Venice.

Not everyone knows of the existence of the monumental Frari cloister, which can be visited by request. The Archivio di Stato occupies the immense rooms of what was one of the vastest monastic complexes of the Serenissima. The eighteenth-century boiseries of the old library of the Franciscans are still found in the large room above the sacristy of the Basilica dei Frari.

CHIESA DI SAN CASSIAN
CHAPEL OF SAN CARLO BORROMEO

Probably built in the tenth century, the Church of San Cassian was restored and rearranged several times, most recently in the latter half of the eighteenth century.

There are three important paintings by Tintoretto in the main chapel.

The famous altarpiece by Antonello da Messina, now at the Kunsthistorisches Museum of Vienna, was kept in this church until the late seventeenth century.

A door halfway down the left aisle of the sacristy affords access to an unusual chapel consecrated to St. Carlo Borromeo. In 1746, a wealthy gentleman, Carlo del Medico, had the small but refined chapel built in pure rococo style, with a profusion of marble and semiprecious stones set in the balustrade and altar frontal.

Some of the furnishings, such as the *prie-dieux* on either side of the altar, are of polychrome marble; the floor is elegantly inlaid with polychrome marble with geometric motifs.

The altarpiece with the Virgin with putto and Saints Carlo Borromeo and Filippo Neri is a work signed and dated by Giovan Battista Pittoni. The ceiling fresco is attributed to the same artist.

SCUOLA GRANDE DI SAN ROCCO
BOISERIE BY FRANCESCO PIANTA

The Scuola Grande of San Rocco was founded in 1478. The construction of the impressive building got underway in 1515 and was completed by Scarpagnino.

In 1576, Tintoretto was commissioned to execute his famous fresco cycles. The lower parts of the walls of a room on the upper floor are decorated with exceptional boiserie by Francesco Pianta the Younger, celebrated sculptor of the seventeenth century. On the long ornamental scroll borne by Mercury, to the right of the arch of the staircase, is a description of the scheme that guided the artist. The order of the figures begins from the east wall; going clockwise, the first figure is Melancholy followed by Honor, Avarice with his accounting books, Ignorance with the head of an ass, Knowledge and the Distinction between Good and Evil. Between the figures of the Fury chained and Curiosity cloaked, there is an enigmatic bookcase with sixty-four volumes of exceptional realism. By the bust of Scandal, we see the allegory of Noble Pleasures symbolized by musical instruments; completing the wall is the figure of Cicero, defender of sculpture, and a caricature of Tintoretto, defender of painting. Lining the walls are twenty-three magnificent lanterns of the eighteenth century, decorated with glass canes.

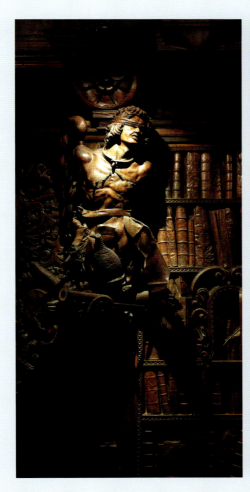

SANTA CROCE

Right from the earliest days, the city of Venice was divided into quarters known as *sestieri*, symbolized by the six metal teeth of the gondola's prow. La Giudecca was considered part of the Dorsoduro *sestiere*.

The Sestiere of Santa Croce, the city's smallest in size, takes its name from an ancient church of the same name, probably founded around the ninth century amid uncultivated marshy lowlands and vegetable gardens. Only at the beginning of the twelfth century, with the arrival of Benedictine monks, was the temple rebuilt and a large monastery erected. The surrounding areas were reclaimed, and the *sestiere* progressively acquired a more urban form with well-defined borders along the Grand Canal and the various internal canals.

In 1470 the monastery went to Franciscan nuns. According to accounts of the time, the friars were turned out because of leading "a rather relaxed and scandalous life." The whole complex was demolished in 1810 under French rule. In the same area, the Counts Papadopoli created a romantic park landscaped by famous set designer Francesco Bagnara. Part of the park was sacrificed in the 1930s in the excavation of the Rio Novo. For many centuries some guilds of wool and fabric dyers were located along the narrow canals of Santa Croce.

Campo della Lana, the Rio dei Tentori, and the Rio dei Garzoti are places whose names testify to the activities carried on there in past times. The *sestiere* is characterized by the presence of grand palazzi built on the banks of minor canals, such as Palazzo Mocenigo in San Stae, and Palazzi Gradenigo and Soranzo Cappello in the Rio Marin, the latter two famous for their vast gardens described by Henry James and Gabriele d'Annunzio, while some of the city's most impressive buildings overlook the Grand Canal, such as Ca' Pesaro, a grand abode designed by Baldassare Longhena, and Ca' Corner della Regina, where Catherine, Queen of Cyprus, was born.

In the Sestiere di Santa Croce are found some of Venice's oldest churches, such as that consecrated to San Giovanni Decollato, called San Zandegolà in Venetian dialect, built in a wonderful square, happily always deserted. The churches of San Simeon Grando and of San Giacomo dell'Orio likewise boast remote origins and conserve valuable artworks unknown to most people. The renowned university of architecture Istituto Universitario di Architettura is housed in the former Monastery dei Tolentini.

PALAZZO GRADENIGO
ON THE RIO MARIN

The origins of Palazzo Gradenigo go back to the middle of the sixteenth century. In the second half of the seventeenth century, the Gradenigo, one of Venice's oldest and most illustrious patrician families, decided to double the size of the building, assigning the extension project to the best-known architect of the period: Baldassare Longhena, the same person who designed the Basilica della Salute. Upon Longhena's death, the project was carried out by his pupil, Domenico Margutti. One enters Palazzo Gradenigo from the quay of the same name through a neoclassical archway, probably designed by Giannantonio Selva, topped by panoplies of triumphant sculpted bearers of arms. A first court follows, adorned by stone pillars and a flight of steps toward the canal bank. Through the ivy-screened apertures in the wall forming a backdrop to the court, one can glimpse what remains of the famed garden. Going on through Longhena's portal, we come to the inner courtyard, where a large statue of the goddess Minerva keeps watch over the main entrance and entrance hall, which is embellished by Istrian stone columns and by the lantern of a Venetian galley, called *fano'*, dating from the early eighteenth century. This large building has three inner courtyards with three well-curbs, three different stairways, and two main floors. The estate was famous for its collections of paintings, for its rich library, and especially for its garden, which, until 1922, was the city's largest. Bull hunts were organized there during the Carnival of 1768, as well as some memorable fetes in honor of the Counts of the north (Czar Pavel and Marie Fedorovna) and of Eugèné de Beauharnais, then viceroy of Italy. In the late nineteenth century, Gabriele d'Annunzio set part of his famous and scandalous novel, *The Flame*, amid the shrubbery of Gradenigo Park. At almost the same time, Henry James set *The Aspern Papers* in the adjoining garden. There was a riding track and stable in the Gradenigo Garden. In 1750 no less than thirty horses were kept there, as well as some carriages. Between World War I and World War II, part of the palazzo was sold and divided into apartments, and the large park was halved and confiscated by the Fascist regime to be used to build a new quarter for housing railroad workers. The wing of the first main floor, overlooking the Rio Marin, was recently restored by the author and decorated with stuccos and frescoes of different periods. The walls of the entrance and dining room are a triumph of the art of Venetian stuccowork circa 1730; notable among the yellow-and-green stucco elements are certain floral details that recall the famed Cordova embossed leatherwork, all the rage in seventeenth-century Venice. Within large oval frames, some scenes of rural life and of the holiday season are frescoed, in grisaille works by the atelier of Giacomo Guarana. The empire room was so redecorated on the occasion of the visit of Viceroy Eugène de Beauharnais in 1807, while the yellow salon features a lovely ceiling frescoed by Guarana, depicting the triumph of Flora, rediscovered during the recent restoration work. Other rooms are decorated with frescoes by Bevilacqua and Borsato.

What remains today of the Gradenigo Garden, restored in 2001, is less than one-fourth its original size. A white wisteria pergola acts as a backdrop to the garden, mirrored by a grape pergola on the opposite side, toward the canal. In the middle an old *Sophora japonica* of the 1920s resembles a green fountain. Two long flowerbeds run along the palazzo and the boundary wall delimiting the gravel pathways that surround the central lawn; these flowerbeds were designed as English-style borders, where a variety of aromatic perennials, typical of the Venetian lagoon garden, bloom from May to October. The wisteria pergola is regularly trimmed according to the topiary art. When likewise planted in 2001, the tall cypresses measured just three meters. The central lawn has a simple rectangular design with the corners rounded off with a quarter circle, as often is the case with the sections of uniform colors used for Venetian terrazzo flooring.

Today, after years of careful restoration work, the palazzo is reviving the ancient tradition of Venetian hospitality.

In the austere entrance hall of Palazzo Gradenigo, decorated with pillars of Istrian stone, are found some family heirlooms and pieces of Venetian history, such as the sixteenth-century wooden coats of arms of the Pesaro and Gradenigo families, and a large ship's lantern.

The rooms of the residence were decorated in different periods and styles. The empire room is furnished with furniture produced at the turn of the nineteenth century. The light fixture is Genovese. The frescoes have been attributed to Davide Rossi.

CASINO TRON
OF THE THEATRE OF SAN CASSIANO

The Theatre of San Cassiano, inaugurated in 1637 and the first public theater in Europe, took its name from the nearby parish church. Of masonry construction, it was built where a previous wooden theater, destroyed by fire in 1629, once stood. Owned by the patrician Tron family of Venice, it was considered "public" since it was directed by an impresario and attended by a paying audience. During the seventeenth century, opera became one of the city's leading attractions. Shortly after the opening of the new theater, nobleman Ettore Tron wrote in his tax return: "A place for acting that at present yields naught." Some of the behavior of the theatergoers is memorable: at the appearance of their favorite singer or actress, they would recite poems and sing praises, releasing white doves from the boxes and tossing flowers and sweets. During an evening in honor of étoile Margherita Grisellini—a famous mid-eighteenth-century ballerina—pheasants, ducks, and partridges were launched from the boxes down to the stalls, and the showpiece on stage turned into a hunt. Built in the shape of a horseshoe with five tiers of boxes, the theater was demolished in 1812. The garden of Palazzo Albrizzi is now planted on its ruins.

Casino Tron, which miraculously survived the demolition, was a freestanding building completely apart from the theater at the time, used as a foyer and gathering place for entertainment and gaming during the intervals of the shows and otherwise. Nearly all the rooms of this rare building are decorated with eighteenth-century polychrome stuccos. A suite of rooms on the long side overlook the silent garden, while an external access way, built of Istrian stone, was probably designed to avoid the disturbance caused by people coming and going from one room to the next. A corner room is frescoed with some scenes of the myth of Apollo, painted in the style of Tiepolo by Costantino Cedini toward the end of the eighteenth century; the elegant stuccos and panels have a Louis Seize flavor. The current owners have carefully restored the old decorations and maintain this timeless dwelling in an exemplary manner.

All the rooms of Casino Tron are decorated with stuccos and
marmorino *plaster dating from the first half of the eighteenth century,*
with colors typical of the period.

*A corner room was elegantly frescoed in the late eighteenth century
by Costantino Cedini, with mythological subjects and allegories.
The walls of the small* portego *(opposite) are decorated
in* marmorino *plaster.*

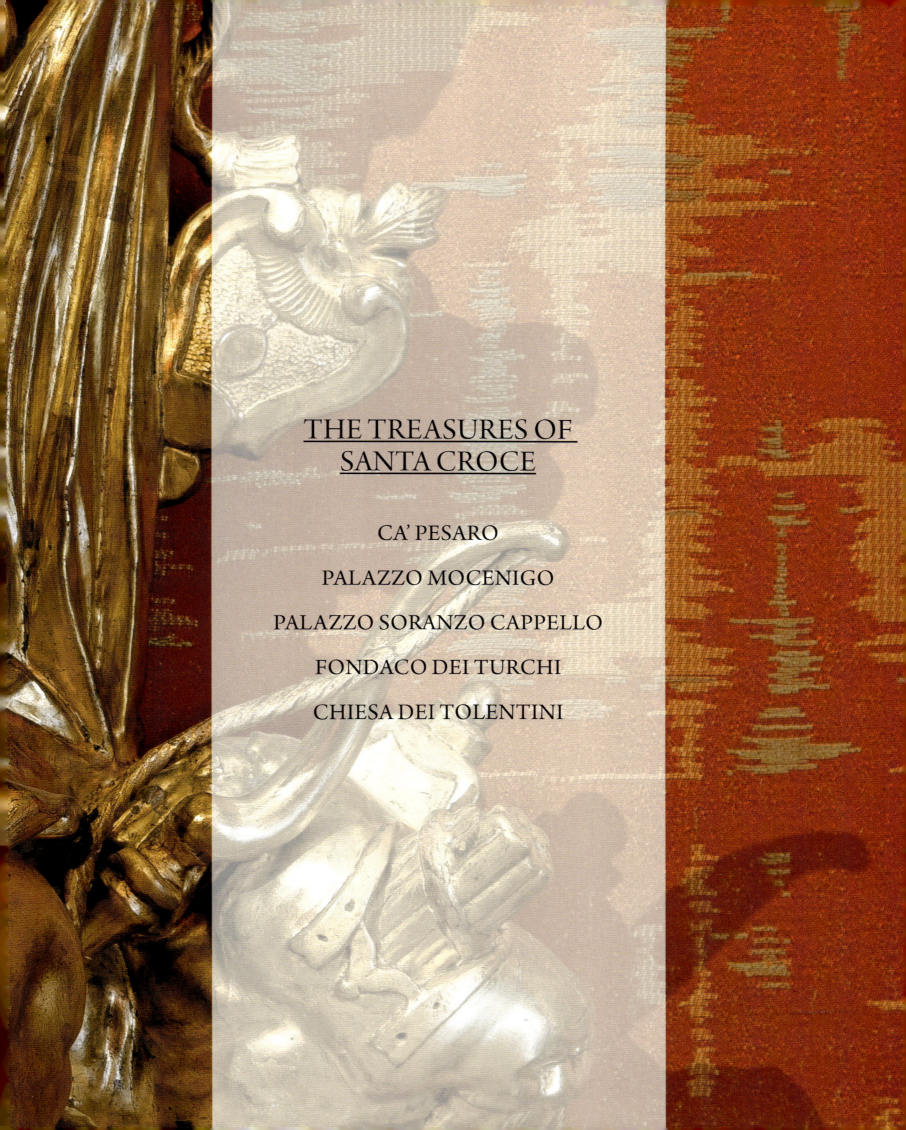

THE TREASURES OF SANTA CROCE

CA' PESARO

PALAZZO MOCENIGO

PALAZZO SORANZO CAPPELLO

FONDACO DEI TURCHI

CHIESA DEI TOLENTINI

CA' PESARO
MUSEUM OF MODERN ART

Ca' Pesaro is perhaps the most extensive, imposing, and sumptuous patrician palazzo of Venice. Starting in 1550, the Pesaro family began to acquire different properties between the Pergola and Due Torri canals.

Moneyed Giovanni Pesaro, doge from 1658 to 1659, commissioned the most celebrated architect of the age, Baldassarre Longhena, to design a grand palazzo for his family between said canals. Work began on the ground level entrance and courtyard, where the beautiful, monumental well-curb designed by Sansovino is found (coming from the courtyard of Palazzo della Zecca, now a reading room of the Marciana National Library) and proceeded until the completion of the facade of the first main floor on the Grand Canal in 1679. Longhena's demise in 1682 marked the suspension of the work for twenty years until architect Antonio Gaspari, a pupil of Longhena, was assigned by Leonardo Pesaro, the doge's nephew, to complete the work following the original plan of the master. In an engraving of 1710, Coronelli shows us the completed facade of the palazzo on the Grand Canal. The exceptional, monumental facade on the very narrow Canale delle Due Torri is entirely made of Istrian stone, following the gentle bend of the canal. Leonardo Pesaro, who would become Procuratore of San Marco, continued to embellish the interior of the building, commissioning frescoes, stuccos, and precious wood carvings. During the nineteenth century, the palazzo changed hands several times until it was finally purchased by Giuseppe La Masa, a general and duke, and his wife, Felicita Bevilacqua. In 1889 the duchess gave the palazzo to the city of Venice on the condition that it would continue to protect and promote little-known artists and "impoverished young art students." Thus came into being the Fondazione Bevilaqua La Masa, a foundation still active today under the arcades of the Procuratorie Nove on Piazza San Marco. The modern art collection, started in 1897 in conjunction with the second edition of the Biennale Internazionale d'Arte, was moved to Ca' Pesaro in 1902. Works by such young artists as Casorati, Boccioni, Gino Rossi, Arturo Martini, and Medardo Rosso were purchased. In time, the collection was enriched by further acquisitions and by donations. In the 1960s, thanks to the Lisi legacy, the museum acquired artworks by Kandinsky, Mirò, Morandi, de Chirico, Chagall, Carrà, and many others. Likewise notable is the collection of nineteenth-century Venetian paintings. Not to be overlooked are the romantic views by Ippolito Caffi. In more recent years the museum received an important donation of sculptures by Adolf Wildt. On the top floor of the palazzo is the State Museum of Oriental Art, where the collection of Enrico di Borbone-Parma is displayed, claimed by Italy as part of war reparations in the aftermath of the victory over Austria in World War I. Even today the museum layout by Nino Barbantini, done between World War I and World War II, feels timeless.

The main stairway of Ca' Pesaro, with its inlaid polychrome marble flooring, amazes with its grandeur and richness. In the portego on the main floor, some eighteenth-century Italian sculptures are displayed amid walls with pilasters and over doors with oval stucco frames.

Some works by Alberto Viani and Adolfo Wildt finally have been placed in the large salon of the new director of the Fondazione Musei Civici of Venice, Gabriella Belli.

PALAZZO MOCENIGO
TEXTILE MUSEUM

The Mocenigo family gave seven doges to the Serenissima, second only to the eight of the Contarini, and distinguished itself over the centuries due to active participation in the military and political life of the Republic of Venice.

In the sixteenth century, the family divided into several branches, with the main branch remaining in the four palazzi in San Samuele. The branch, called San Stae—after the church of the same name near the palazzo—had the building erected in the late sixteenth century. Ample three-light windows, called *serliane*, characterize the nearly identical front and back, on the Rio di San Stae and on the *salizzada*. The conformation of the house is in keeping with the features proper to Venice's patrician homes, with the large *portego* going down the middle with rooms to either side, even if a vast wing was added on the canal, creating a striking enfilade of rooms. The interior was redecorated a number of times, memorably in 1787, when some ceilings were frescoed by Giacomo Guarana, Giambattista Canal, and Giovanni Scajaro on occasion of the wedding of Alvise Mocenigo to Laura Corner. The walnut burl door panels are exquisite; likewise noteworthy is the fineness of some pieces of grand, carved, and gilded furniture crafted by Veneto carvers, close to the art of famed Antonio Corradini. Count Nicolò Mocenigo donated the palazzo to the municipality of Venice to be made into a museum to complete the Correr Museum.

In 1985, after major restoration work, the Mocenigo apartment was opened to the public. In the same year, the Centro Studi di Storia del Tessuto e del Costume was founded, which features ample collections of textiles and clothes of former times of the civic museums, mainly coming from the Correr, Guggenheim, Cini, and Grassi collections, as well as a specialized library. The visit to the museum—completely renovated and enlarged in 2013—comprises twenty rooms on the main floor, doubling the exhibition space opened in 1985. Taken together, the rooms form a whole, evoking the different facets of the lives and activities of Venice's patrician class between the seventeenth and eighteenth centuries and are populated by manikins wearing precious garments and antique accessories belonging to the center.

The recent restoration was done under the enlightened direction of scene designer Pier Luigi Pizzi, who managed to restore the elegance and splendor of eighteenth-century Venice to this grand patrician residence.

PALAZZO SORANZO CAPPELLO

In the latter half of the sixteenth century, the Bragadin family undertook a major renovation of a complex situated on the Rio Marin, also known as Dei Garzoti.

The year 1612 marks the death of Giacomo Bragadin, who probably commissioned the first conspicuous extension of the palazzo, which was then auctioned off to Lorenzo Soranzo. The Soranzo family began work on a series of projects, adding a wing to the palazzo on the Rio Marin, and an impressive garden. Both palazzo and garden appear finished in the engraving by Vincenzo Coronelli of 1709, where one appreciates the French-style parterre layout of the garden and the west facade of the palazzo, below which is a singular courtyard, adorned by statues depicting the Caesars.

In 1788, after this branch of the Soranzo died out, the complex went to the Cappello family. By 1880 the palazzo and garden were owned by Contessa Carlotta Cavalli di Trento. Described by Henry James in *The Aspern Papers*, in the late nineteenth century it was actually rented in part to Mrs. Constance Fletcher, a writer under the penname of George Fleming, who lived there together with her stepfather, painter Eugene Benson, and her elderly mother. Even d'Annunzio, in the *Taccuini* and then in *The Flame*, chose Palazzo Soranzo Cappello, its garden, and that of adjoining Palazzo Gradenigo for some scenes of the famous novel. The estate was later bought by the state and restored by the Italian Ministry of Culture. Today, it is the seat of two superintendencies. The garden may be visited.

FONDACO DEI TURCHI
MUSEUM OF NATURAL HISTORY

Erected in the thirteenth century by the Pesaro, the palazzo was purchased in 1381 by the Repubblica Serenissima, which gave it to Marchese Nicolò V of Ferrara as a token of gratitude for the help he gave the republic during the War of Chioggia against the Genoese. Hence the old name "home of the Duke of Ferrara."

In 1438 the seigniory asked the d'Este to give hospitality to the emperor of Constantinople, Giovanni Paleologo. Torquato Tasso stayed here in the retinue of Duke Alfonso d'Este, who had come to meet with Henry III, King of France and Poland.

In 1621, after the property had changed hands a number of times, the Serenissima reserved the use of the building to the Ottomans, who made it their headquarters, which is to say, a warehouse for the traders of the whole Ottoman Empire. The last Turkish resident left the palazzo in 1838, when Venice was no longer the capital of an independent state but a province of the Hapsburg Empire.

John Ruskin drew some details of the facade of the building in ruinous condition in 1850. In 1858, the municipality of Venice bought the palazzo, shortly thereafter assigning its restoration to architect Federico Berchet, who interpreted more than restored the building in Veneto-Byzantine Revival style.

It was the seat of the Correr Museum from 1880 until 1922, at which time the collection was moved to Procuratie Nuove on Piazza San Marco. It is currently the home of the Museum of Natural History.

Notwithstanding the evident late nineteenth-century reworking, the facade, rich in polychrome marble and anthropomorphic reliefs, offers a rare example of the medieval Venetian palazzo.

Sharply criticized as exemplifying an "overly restored" building at the end of the nineteenth century, Fondaco dei Turchi, especially at night, appears as a dreamlike vision of old Byzantine Venice.

CHIESA DEI TOLENTINI
MONUMENT TO PATRIARCH MOROSINI

The Church of Tolentini was based on a design by architect Vincenzo Scamozzi at the end of the sixteenth century and completed a century later by Andrea Tirali, who, inspired by Palladio's style, added a stately pronaos with tympanum and six Corinthian columns to the facade.

Of particular interest is the funerary monument dedicated to the patriarch of Venice, Giovan Francesco Morosini, a work by Genoese sculptor Filippo Parodi (1630–1702). Parodi had come to Venice after some time in Rome, where, beginning from 1655 he worked for six years with Cavalier Bernini. Cardinal Morosini was born in Venice in 1604 and in 1644 he was elected patriarch of Venice by the senate by a vast majority.

Against the background of the burdensome Candia war, he held office for thirty-four years, making his the longest patriarchate in the history of the Republic.

In 1677, Parodi opened shop in Venice.

One of his first pupils was a young wood carver from Belluno, Andrea Brustolon.

Soon after, work began on the magnificent funerary monument dedicated to Patriarch Morosini, located on the left wall of the main chapel of the temple dedicated to San Nicola da Tolentino.

The composition of this well-organized, virtuoso baroque-stage sets, magnificently sculpted and modeled (the pall and the putti are stucco), clearly harks back to Bernini's Roman models, even if one can already see hints of early rococo elements.

Found in the little-visited Church of Tolentini, celebrated for its pronaos with a colonnade inspired by the Pantheon of Rome, is a series of important examples of sculpture and painting. The details of the monument sculpted by Parodi reveal knowledge of the techniques in use in the city of the popes.

CASTELLO

The quarter takes its name from a castle probably built by the first Veneto people who had come to the lagoon in flight from the hinterland in search of defense against barbarian invaders. The fortress rose on Olivolo, the island upon where the Basilica of San Pietro of Castello was later built, which, until 1807, was the bishop's seat of the Republic.

The Arsenale, built in the twelfth century, was Europe's largest shipyard of the time, surrounded by walls and battlements. In the periods of peak production, more than sixteen thousand workers were employed here. One enters from the Renaissance portal built in 1460, with watch kept by a pack of ancient lions coming from Greece, landed in the lagoon as booty.

In recent years, part of the Arsenale has been renovated to house the exhibits of the Bienniale of Venice, the glorious institution founded more than a century ago with the aim of promoting the contemporary visual arts. Not far from the Arsenale, the equestrian monument of Capitano Colleoni, Verrocchio's masterpiece, stands tall on the high pedestal in front of the Basilica of Santi Giovanni e Paolo, the mass of which dominates the north side of the *sestiere* of Castello.

A real pantheon of the Serenissima, the basilica contains numerous monuments sculpted to celebrate doges, captains, and condottieri. Located not far from Riva degli Schiavoni is spacious and quiet Campo della Bragora, with its little-known fifteenth-century church, where it is possible to admire some masterpieces by Cima da Conegliano and by the Vivarini. In the vicinity, on the Rio della Pietà, is the Scuola Dalamata di San Giorgio e Trifonone, renowned for the pictorial cycle executed by Vittore Carpaccio. The Greek community, present in Venice ever since the beginning of the thirteenth century, also built a Scuola and a church, the latter of which is famous for the important Byzantine icons kept there. Nearby, architect Mauro Codussi built his masterwork: the facade of the Church of San Zaccaria, completed in the sixteenth century.

Located in the most remote area of the *sestiere* of Castello is the church dedicated to San Francesco della Vigna, rebuilt by Jacopo Sansovino in 1534 by will of Doge Andrea Gritti, who had his palazzo opposite the front of the church. The Castello neighborhood is characterized by the presence of important monumental architectures that coexist with modest homes strung with an abundance of clotheslines between one narrow street and the next, between a waterway and deserted Fondamenta exposed to the sun.

A RESIDENCE IN THE SHADOW
OF THE WALLS OF THE ARSENALE

The canal, the Fondamenta, and Campo delle Gorne take their names from the large roof gutters, *gorne* in Veneto dialect, of Istrian stone, which collect the rainwater from the pitched roofs of the old yards of the Arsenale and pour it into the canal below the crenulated walls. Over twenty years ago, in this remote area of Venice, an elegant lady purchased three small houses, considered minor buildings that were in terrible condition. The three buildings did not relate to one another, and stood around a small inner garden in a state of neglect. Prolonged restoration work turned the three little houses into a single home, with a lovely terrace that overlooks the Rio delle Gorne. The materials used for the restoration work were the same used for centuries around the lagoon, such as for the Venetian *terrazzo* terrace and the ceiling beams. Lemons and jasmine thrive in the garden protected by the monumental walls of the Arsenale. Artist Oriel Harewood has devised a set of white furniture sculpted for the front hall, allegorically drawing on certain architectural, historical, and landscape elements tied to Venetian tradition.

CASA MIANI
IN SAN PIETRO DI CASTELLO

Tradition has it that the first inhabitants of the lagoon planted olive orchards in this remote island of the city.

Other sources contend that the name "Olivolo" derives from the olive shape of the island itself. In 1091, it became the seat of the first bishop of the Venetians, who assumed the title of Vescovo Olivolense, while in 1451, after the unification of the patriarchates of Grado and Venice, it became the seat of the patriarchate of Venice, which it remained until 1807. The Cathedral of San Pietro boasts ancient origins. Rebuilt several times over the centuries, it features a classical facade in the style of Palladio, dating from 1596. The bell tower, designed by Mauro Codussi in 1482, is the only one in the city made entirely of Istrian stone. The Palazzo Patriarcale, likewise rebuilt in the late sixteenth century, was reduced to barracks from 1807 until World War II.

The island slowly deteriorated owing to the crisis of the Arsenale shipyards, and only recently is it rediscovering its identity, mainly thanks to the restoration of the Arsenale, promoted by the Venice Biennale.

As is true of all the lagoon islands with monumental ecclesiastic complexes, the island of San Pietro di Castello had a building with a cavana, or boathouse, to shelter docked boats.

But all traces of this building had been lost. Only thanks to the courageous restoration work undertaken by Giorgio and Ilaria Miani was it possible to rediscover the original vault of the cavana of the patriarch, which had been walled up and subdivided. Above the cavana is a two-story building, with a typical Veneto dormer terminating in a gable. The house was in a terrible state and had been marred by a countless mishmash of projects. The building has been admirably restored, thanks to the expertise of the new owners, who are specialized in reclaiming historic homes.

HOTEL METROPOLE

Beginning from 1703, famed composer and violinist Antonio Vivaldi was choirmaster and violin teacher of Ospedale della Pietà, an ancient institution that took in orphan girls and trained them in music. The fifteenth-century Church della Pietà and Oratorio annex were demolished in 1745 to make way for the construction of a new complex designed by architect Giorgio Massari, finished in 1760.

The Hotel Metropole stands on the site once occupied by Vivaldi's renowned Oratorio.

Only a few are aware that the pillars that decorate the present-day hotel bar once adorned the oratory where the virtuoso *rosso* (redheaded) maestro used to practice with the young orphan girls. For years the nineteenth-century building we see today has been housing the elegant hotel, brilliantly run by Gloria Beggiato, a well-known collector of ivories, fans, and Venetian gifts and fancy goods, who has transformed part of the hotel entrance into a small but precious museum. The hotel's restaurant is famous for having received a Michelin star.

In the elegant dining room of the Hotel Metropole, two wooden angels, dating from the beginning of the seventeenth century, decorate the niches on either side of the fireplace. Only in Venice do hotels and homes alike have two entrances—one from land, the other from water. In Venice the wooden poles used to dock boats are painted with the colors of the coat of arms of the family that owns the building.

THE TREASURES OF CASTELLO

CA' GRIMANI IN SANTA MARIA FORMOSA

OSPEDALETTO

MUSEO STORICO NAVALE

CHIESA DI SAN MARTINO

CHIESA DI SAN FRANCESCO DELLA VIGNA

CA' GRIMANI IN SANTA MARIA FORMOSA
STATE MUSEUM

In 2001, the Ministry of Italian Culture entrusted the care for Palazzo Grimani, purchased by the state in 1981, to the State Musueums of Venice.

For the city of Venice, the palazzo, recently reopened following major restoration work, constitutes an especially precious novelty of international importance owing to the originality of its architecture, its decoration, and the history of events that have characterized it. In the early sixteenth century, Antonio Grimani gave his children the palazzo; the complex was later completed thanks to grandson Giovanni, patriarch of Aquileia, and his brother Vettore, Procuratore of San Marco. It is likely that the same Grimani heirs played a part in the planning and decorating of the palazzo.

The architecture blends Tosco-Roman and Venetian elements: the Tribuna, previously seat of the renowned archaeological collection of Giovanni Grimani (now kept in the Tribuna of the Marciana Biblioteca Nazionale), the Roman-style courtyard, and the exquisite stairway are particularly suggestive. The decorative pictures and stuccos are exceptional. As had previously been the case with architecture, the Grimani turned to artists with a Roman background: Giovanni da Udine, pupil of Raphael; Francesco and Giuseppe Salviati; Camillo Mantovano; and Federico Zuccari.

All this makes Palazzo Grimani a unique building in terms of the history and architecture of Venice, fascinating for cultural, artistic, and historic reasons and finally opened as a museum in and of itself, plus a few highly select works exemplifying the taste of collectors in sixteenth-century Venice.

The wrought-iron gate of the water door probably goes back to the seventeenth century. The palazzo's monumental and unusual land entrance is adorned by sculptures dating from Roman times. The "antiquities room," or the room where the most precious sculptures of the collection of the patriarch of Aquileia were displayed, is lit by a large square skylight above the vaults, which later are decorated with elegant stucco coffers. The classical sculptural group depicting the rape of Ganymede was recently returned to its original place.

Antinoo, the favorite of Emperor Hadrian, is portrayed in a splendid marble bust of the second century AD that belonged to Giovanni Grimani.

On several occasions the portals and the fireplaces of this rich sixteenth-century dwelling, built using old marble, have been attributed to Sanmicheli and to Palladio. The vault of the grand stairway leading to the main floor is decorated with stuccos by Giovanni da Udine.

The frescoed grotesques, rediscovered during recent restoration work, draw on the decorations conceived by Raphael for the Vatican loggias.

Some elegant stucco baskets decorate the vaults of the loggias on the ground floor.

A fabulous pergola, frescoed by Camillo Mantovano, beautifies one of the main

floor salons. In a small vaulted room, Francesco Salviati painted scenes from the myth of Apollo.

In the middle of the ceiling, Giovanni da Udine executed a stucco Apollo driving his chariot.

OSPEDALETTO
MUSIC HALL

The Church of Santa Maria dei Derelitti, called Ospedaletto, was built on the site of an old hospital. Reworked a number of times down through the centuries, the exterior is now distinguished by a complex baroque facade based on a design by Baldassarre Longhena in 1674.

In the mid-seventeenth century, architect Giuseppe Sardi extended the structure of the old hospital adjoining the church and built a pretty ovoid stairway, inspired by one built a century before by Palladio for the Convento della Carità, now Gallerie dell'Accademia.

Already in the seventeenth century, "the chorus of the daughters of the Pio Ospitale dei Derelitti nearby SS. Giovanni e Paolo"—poor orphan girls housed in the adjoining Ospedaletto—used to give rousing performances in this temple to a large following.

The success of the musical events led to the construction of the Sala della Musica (music hall) designed in 1776 by little-known Matteo Lucchesi and entirely frescoed by Giacomo Guarana, with trompe l'oeil architectural quadratures executed by Agostino Mengozzi Colonna.

Important concerts were held in this elegant room with curvilinear walls. In the little choir above the main entrance, the young orphan girls would perform behind the grating visible to the sides of the hall, repeated in trompe l'oeil on the opposite side over the lacquered doors.

On the back wall, a fresco depicts Apollo and the Muses in concert.

This is one of the exceedingly rare oval rooms of Venice. Agostino Mengozzi Colonna, of the famed family of fresco painters from Emilia specialized in three-dimensional rendering of architecture, was inspired by works executed by his father for the ballroom of Palazzo Labia.

MUSEO STORICO NAVALE
PADIGLIONE DELLE NAVI

Founded in 1919 after World War I, the museum is quartered in a fifteenth-century building that was one of the old granaries of the Republic of Venice.

Added in 1977 to the preexistent Museo Storico Navale (naval museum), the Padiglione delle Navi occupies 2,000 square meters, just a few steps away from the main entrance of the historic Arsenale. In 1577 a huge fire temporarily forced the members of the Maggior Consiglio to meet in these vast pavilions instead of the Palazzo Ducale. On display in the three-section museum are a Baglietto Asso racing boat, speed champion in 1932; a work steamboat of 1895, with the coal-fired boilers in plain sight; and a royal motorboat built by Celli in 1929.

In the middle of the second section is the *scalè reale*, a stupendous eighteen-oar craft with cabin and hull adorned by golden sculptures and friezes. It was built in the Arsenale around 1850 and utilized for the most solemn ceremonies of those years. All around are gondolas and small *bragozzi* (fishing boats), in addition to a vast collection of other craft of the Venetian lagoon. A standout in the last pavilion is the engine section of Guglielmo Marconi's *Elettra*, with its huge boilers.

Built in 1904 for Archduke Karl Stephan of Hapsburg, it became known as the great scientist's floating laboratory; it was from here in 1930 that the signal was given that turned on the lights of Sydney, 25,000 kilometers away. And still more rowboats and sailboats, friezes, and reliefs of St. Mark's lions, which adorned the walls of Venice's fortresses, make these rooms unique.

CHIESA DI SAN MARTINO

The foundation of the church dedicated to St. Martin of Tours goes back to the early Middle Ages. In the famous view etched by de' Barbari in 1500, one sees a building with a typically Veneto-Byzantine layout.

In 1540, Jacopo Sansovino, *proto*, or architect, in charge of the maintenance and restoration of the Basilica of San Marco, was assigned the job of building the new temple.

He opted for a square layout. In later centuries, the church was enhanced by wall frescoes and by the monument to Doge Erizzo. The organ is located over the entrance portal; the choir is decorated with a large canvas executed in 1549 by Gerolamo da Santacroce. The painting is held up by a pair of wooden angels magnificently carved in 1737 by Matteo Calderoni, a little-known artist recently rediscovered, thanks to the restoration of the *Bucintoro* (the old Venetian state barge) of the Savoy, fashioned by him. There is an elegant early Renaissance altar in this temple that came from the destroyed Church of the Santo Sepolcro; it was crafted by Tullio Lombardo in 1484, in imitation of the Holy Sepulcher of Jerusalem.

CHIESA DI SAN FRANCESCO DELLA VIGNA

The complex of the Franciscan Minorites rose in 1253 on vineyards donated to the friars by Marco Ziani, son of Doge Pietro.

The old temple was built with a nave without side aisles, and a chorus for the friars, in all likelihood situated in the middle of the church (as still is that of the Basilica dei Frari). The Lombardo-style front of the choir with marble reliefs depicting prophets and evangelists now decorates the walls of the Badoer-Giustinian Chapel, built along with the new temple by Jacopo Sansovino in 1534. The great Florentine architect and sculptor, tasked by Doge Andrea Gritti, likewise provided no side aisles but included side chapels and an ample main chapel where the elegant funerary monuments of the Gritti are situated. One of the side chapels on the left was rebuilt in 1743 by architect Temanza for the hugely wealthy Sagredo family. The whole architecture is sumptuously decorated with Carrara marble sculptures that portray Doge Nicolò Sagredo and his brother, Patriarch Alvise, and with stucco wreaths and monochrome frescoes of the Evangelists painted by Gian Battista Tiepolo. The altar frontal is a magnificent work of marble and semiprecious stone inlays, probably executed by Florentine workers during the first half of the eighteenth century.

DORSODURO

Dorsoduro acts as a divide between the Canale della Giudecca and the Grand Canal. Tradition has it that here there were some islets formed by compact terrain with a few rises. This would explain the origin of the name of the *sestiere* itself, literally "hard rise."

The Basilica della Salute, Longhena's architectural triumph, majestically marks the beginning of the Grand Canal with its hundreds of statues. A short distance away, unfinished Palazzo Venier dei Leoni houses the famous collection of Peggy Guggenheim. The eccentric American collector lived in this residence from 1949 to 1979, collecting leading examples of the visual arts of her time.

A series of facades in different styles follow one after the other all the way to Ca' Foscari, the outer limit of the Dorsoduro quarter, and now seat of the University of Venice. Once, valuable salt was unloaded from ships on to plain wooden rafts to be unloaded again on the Fondamenta delle Zattere landing before being stored in the Magazzini del Sale. The old salt storehouses have since been converted into exhibition spaces.

The salt trade gave rise to the first great fortunes of the merchants of the Serenissima. Some of the city's most important museums are located in this quarter, such as the Gallerie dell'Accademia, where the great masterpieces of Veneto painting are exhibited, and Ca' Rezzonico, focused on eighteenth-century Venetian art, in addition to the abovementioned Guggenheim collection. Not far from the said academy is the Church dei Carmini, where there are two masterpieces—one by Lorenzo Lotto and the other by Cima da Conegliano.

Overlooking the Rio dei Carmini is Ca' Zenobio, one of the city's most impressive palazzi, known for its vast garden and monumental baroque ballroom with a ceiling twice normal height, frescoed by Louis Dorigny. The complex was designed by Antonio Gaspari at the close of the seventeenth century.

The Church of San Sebastiano, a few steps from Palazzo Zenobio, represents the apotheosis of the work of Paolo Veronese, who painted the canvases for the ceiling, the altars, and the splendid but little-known sacristy.

CA' VENDRAMIN AI CARMINI

At the end of the sixteenth century, one branch of the Vendramin, a family of doges, built a palazzo on the Rio dei Carmini, bordering on the grand home of the Foscarini. Each of the two palazzi was known for its sumptuously decorated interior, art collection, library, and extensive garden in back, which partially still exists.

In 1750 many of the palazzo's rooms were redecorated for the occasion of the wedding of Pietro Vendramin to beautiful Fiorenza Ravagnin, who had inherited the fortune of her first husband, Recanati. Giuseppe Angeli, pupil of Piazzetta, frescoed some rooms of the lower main floor.

But the most extraordinarily decorated rooms of this palazzo are on the mezzanine floor, where an enfilade of drawing rooms overlook the canal. Everything is rococo, from the walnut burl doors to the Verona marble fireplaces, large mirrors framed by stuccos, and marvelous tiles painted and gilded in chinoiserie style to depict amorous scenes set in the most lighthearted and fanciful polychrome stuccos ever executed on the lagoon. Here is one of the most significant and complete examples of mid-eighteenth Venetian taste. At the beginning of the twentieth century, poet Henry de Régner stayed in these rooms.

A NINETEENTH-CENTURY
RUSSIAN RESIDENCE AT THE ZATTERE

In the latter half of the nineteenth century, the city of Venice took in some important "outlanders," who bought and renovated grand dwellings.

During summer sojourns, they would organize *salons littéraires* and society events.

From faraway Russia came well-to-do Prince Dolgorouky, who built a villa in neoclassical style, with a garden and terraces on the Fondamenta delle Zattere.

The building is one of a kind, owing above all to the elegant decorations of the rooms on the main floor, which draw on motifs typical of late nineteenth-century Russian taste.

It seems that the wealthy prince had everything sent from St. Petersburg, from parquettes inlaid and trimmed with different types of wood to elaborate doors lacquered white.

Even the sizes of the rooms and arrangements of the windows recall the interiors of Russian mansions overlooking the Neva, and the canals of the Venice of the north, in large part designed by Italian architects. But instead of the slabs of ice that for months hide the waters of Russian rivers, here the glare of the green water of Canal della Giudecca is reflected on the walls and ceilings of the palazzo.

The current residents, refined aesthetes and also "outlanders," have managed to preserve the cosmopolitan spirit of the home, decorating it with furniture and objects from different places.

The dwelling has a lived-in atmosphere amid family portraits, and old and contemporary books. A large Flemish tapestry brightens the far wall. An Aubusson Empire carpet is laid on the Russian parquet.

In the salon, a set of furniture for displaying books is the fruit
of an idea of the master of the house, inspired by some furnishings of
d'Annunzio's Vittoriale. Everything in the small study bespeaks travels,
literature, family heirlooms from other homes, and future projects.

CA' GIUSTINIAN BRANDOLINI

The very old Giustinian family built twin palazzi sometime in the second half of the fifteenth century, probably with the collaboration of Giovanni and Bartolomeo Bon. The aim was to house two branches of the same family: the Giustinians called "dei Vescovi" occupied the palazzo bordering on Ca' Foscari, while the Giustinians "dalle Zoge" lived, until the mid-nineteenth century, in the palazzo currently owned by the Counts Brandolini d'Adda, who purchased it in 1876. Each palazzo has an independent ground entrance and a courtyard surrounded by high crenellated Gothic walls. Some of the rooms on the lower main floor conserve interesting stucco decorations executed by the school of Jacopo Sansovino, and a pictorial cycle by Palma il Giovane. The upper main floor was completely renovated during the latter half of the nineteenth century by the Brandolini d'Addas, who had the *portego* decorated with voluminous stuccos, large mirrors, and parquet in Beaux Arts style. The Gothic stairway outside was demolished to create a terrace at the second floor, while the old Gothic courtyard was extended and a romantic secret garden was planted.

Following pages: Not many years ago, Brando and Cristiana
Brandolini d'Adda undertook major restoration work and interior
decoration in collaboration with Renzo Mongiardino. They also
bought two large canvases by Tiepolo's pupil at the Beistegui auction
at Palazzo Labia, which they brilliantly centered on the salon walls.
The current residents, Paolo and Aud Cuniberti, own an important
collection of Murano glassware produced in the 1930s and 1940s, as
well as contemporary sculptures by Ritsue Mishima, smartly set up in
the middle of the portego.

The walls of one of the palazzo's rooms have been adorned by Renzo Mongiardino with valuable batiks. The walnut doors date from the seventeenth century. The huge mirror gracing a dining room wall probably comes from a Genoa palazzo.

CA' GIUSTINIAN BRANDOLINI D'ADDA

The third and final floor of Palazzo Giustinian Brandolini, with its handsome Gothic four-light window, has been wonderfully converted into a loggia by Brando and Cristiana Brandolini d'Adda, who made good use of the precious collaboration of Renzo Mongiardino. The walls of the loggia are covered with Canadian ivy; gardenias, hydrangeas, and basil flourish there. A small room of this elegant residence is decorated with stuccos probably executed by Ticino master Carpoforo Mazzetti Tencalla around 1740. Allegories of the arts are depicted in relief in the medallions above the mirrors on the walls of a magnificently preserved little boudoir. A delightful rooftop garden has been planted on the terrace on the top floor, where at one time clothes were hung to dry. Marcantonio Giustiunian (1619–1688), the only doge of this very old family, was born in this historic residence. Between 1858 and 1859, Richard Wagner stayed here, and it was here that he composed Act II of *Tristan and Isolde*.

CA' GIUSTINIAN RECANATI

Mention was made of the Giustinian family in Venetian chronicles since the most remote times. The family originated in Istria, even if generous genealogists had them descend directly from Emperor Justinian. They produced numerous procurators, captains, ambassadors, cardinals, and a doge of the Republic of Venice. The family divided into different branches and built numerous palazzi in the city. In 1171, following a tragic naval battle against Byzantine Emperor Manuele I Comneno, all the males in the Giustinian family perished with the sole exception of Nicolò, a monk of the San Nicolò del Lido monastery. It is said that to prevent the extinction of the noble house, Pope Alexander III released Nicolò from his vows and ordered him to wed Anna Michiel, daughter of Doge Vitale. The two scions married and produced numerous descendants. After several years Nicolò went back to his monastery. Once the last of the offspring was weaned, wife Anna took the vows and retired with some of her daughters to the Convent of Sant'Ariano, founded by her.

Palazzo Giustinian alle Zattere was built in the mid-fourteenth century with a sole main floor, even though it occupies the whole area running from Fondamenta delle Zattere to the Rio di Ognissanti, or "one block" as they would say in New York. The facade, with ample stretches of plaster sans architectural flourishes, suggests the former presence of frescoed decoration. In the seventeenth century, prolific architect Longhena designed the majestic portal of the entrance to the portego.

In 1712, Giacomo Giustinian married Laura Recanati, last descendant of a rich and illustrious patrician family, from whom he inherited the important collections of artworks that today can still be admired in the magnificent dwelling, perfectly kept by the current owners, who inherited it from the last descendants of Giustinian–Recanati. At the beginning of the nineteenth century, architect Antonio Diedo designed the new wing of the palazzo with a curious neoclassical exedra that separates the romantic garden from the canal in back.

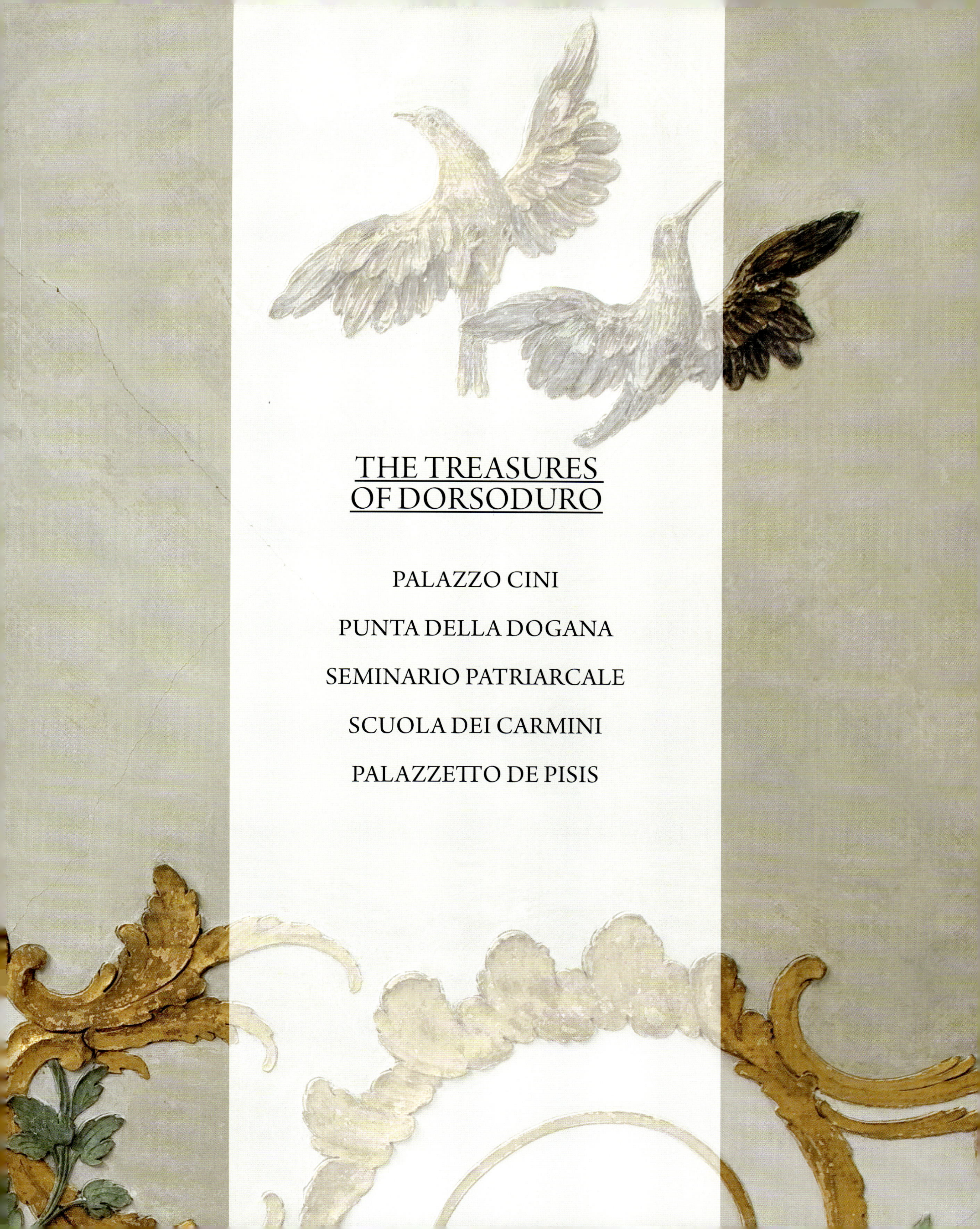

THE TREASURES OF DORSODURO

PALAZZO CINI

PUNTA DELLA DOGANA

SEMINARIO PATRIARCALE

SCUOLA DEI CARMINI

PALAZZETTO DE PISIS

PALAZZO CINI
GIORGIO CINI FOUNDATION

Between 1919 and 1925, Count Vittorio Cini, one of Italy's greatest entrepreneurs of the twentieth century, purchased two sixteenth-century palazzi situated between the Rio di San Vio and the Grand Canal.

The buildings were joined, and the residence became populated with old paintings, glassware, china, and sumptuous furnishings. Vittorio Cini, an enlightened collector, sought advice from art historians, including Bernard Berenson, Federico Zeri, and Giuseppe Fiocco, and from trusted experts such as Nino Barbantini.

In the 1950s the collections kept in the palazzo, grown enormously in the meantime, were reorganized to display the artworks to better advantage.

In 1956, architect Tomaso Buzzi was called on to redesign the interiors of the two Palazzi Cini. He built the elegant spiral staircase and thought up the small oval dining room in rococo-revival style, where he placed an important china service produced by renowned Cozzi of Venice in the latter half of the eighteenth century. In 1977, following Cini's demise, the palazzi of San Vio were again divided among the heirs. In 1981 daughter Yana Alliata di Montereale gave the Giorgio Cini Foundation the palazzo of San Vio, formerly of the Valmarana, and the precious collection of Tuscan Renaissance paintings inherited from her father. Among the masterpieces displayed in this museum are works by Filippo Lippi, Beato Angelico, Botticelli, and Piero di Cosimo, as well as the splendid double portrait by Pontormo, in addition to the collection of early Renaissance paintings from Ferrara.

PUNTA DELLA DOGANA
FRANCOIS PINAULT FOUNDATION

Punta della Dogana, with its triangular shape, separates the Grand Canal from the Canale della Giudecca.

During the fifteenth century, the burgeoning trade of the Serenissima caused the old customhouse in the Castello quarter to be outgrown. A new one was built on the point, then named "del Sale," after the old salt storehouses that still stand in the vicinity on the Fondamenta delle Zattere.

In 1631, the Herculean task of the construction of the Basilica della Salute, designed by Baldassare Longhena, got underway; in 1677, architect Giuseppe Benoni was tasked with completely renovating the Punta structures. Thus, the old fifteenth-century cube-shaped keep was eliminated and replaced by an austere architecture made light by the large rusticated pillars that bear the terraces around the new turret, the tip of which is surmounted by a group of sculptures by Bernardo Falcone da Lugano, featuring a soaring personification of Fortune on a golden globe, borne by two Atlases. At the outset of the nineteenth century, Punta della Dogana underwent various changes and restoration work. In 1835, under Austrian sway, work was begun to enlarge the Magazzini. In 2006, after years of neglect, the city of Venice launched an international competition for the creation of a new art center. The following year the Palazzo Grassi Foundation, headed by Francois Pinault, won the competition with a design by renowned architect Tadao Ando. The magnificent new exhibition space houses rotating selections of contemporary artworks from the François Pinault Foundation collection.

SEMINARIO PATRIARCALE
BIBLIOTECA MONUMENTALE

The stately building was built in 1669 based on a design by Longhena for the congregation of the Somaschi Fathers, abolished in 1810 under French rule.

In 1815, by imperial decree of Francis I of Austria, the complex was assigned to the Patriarchal Seminary, which was located at the old Murano Church of San Cipriano, which is no longer in existence. The Biblioteca Monumentale occupies a huge space twice the normal height on the side facing the Grand Canal. It was built to house the famed library of the Somaschi Fathers, which vanished during French occupation, including the sumptuous carved wooden furnishings. The library's current wood structure, dating from 1817, drew on the shapes of the old library's lost furnishings, albeit adapted to the taste of the time. The library was progressively enriched with works coming from monasteries and convents abolished under French and Austrian domination, and by legacies of the Patriarchs of Venice. Volumes of great bibliographic value are kept here, including a wealth of historical and literary works. In the loft can be admired one large canvas each by Antonio Zanchi, Sebastiano Ricci, and Nicolò Bambini, artists active in Venice in the early eighteenth century.

SCUOLA DEI CARMINI

The Scuola of Charity and Devotion of Santa Maria dei Carmini was recognized by the Council of Ten in 1597.

The purpose of the Scuola was to provide economic and religious support to the members, to dispense alms to the sick and needy, and to procure a dowry for marriageable young women. The first seat stood by the Church and Convent dei Carmini, which at the time belonged to the Order of Our Lady of Mount Carmel. The building was completely rebuilt during the latter half of the seventeenth century based upon a plan by Longhena. The two elegant facades are completely built of Istrian stone. The rooms of the Scuola, spared the looting common to the nineteenth century, still contain the original furnishings, which include important pictorial cycles on canvas, stucco decorations, and boiserie. Between 1739 and 1749, Giambattista Tiepolo painted nine ceiling sections in the Sala del Capitolo (chapter hall). The large central painting represents the *Apparition of Our Lady of Mount Carmel to San Simone Stock as She Consigns Him the Scapular*, which is surrounded by magnificent stuccowork done by Abbondio Stazio and Carpoforo Mazzetti Tencalla. The archive and meeting rooms are likewise elegantly decorated with rare polychrome marble flooring and splendid carved woodwork. The vaults of the stairway and the unusual corridor that joins the two flights are decorated with ornate polychrome stuccos. The Scuola, still sustained by its confraternity, is open to the public, and houses various cultural events.

PALAZZETTO DE PISIS
VENETIAN HERITAGE FOUNDATION

In 1943, Ferrara painter Filippo de Pisis bought the small Gothic palazzo that overlooks the Rio di San Sebastiano.

The artist turned the residence into a combination home and atelier, where he worked until 1953. The original building, dating from the second half of the fifteenth century, probably was left unfinished, which would explain the sole main floor and the disproportionate size of the central triple lancet window viewed against the low facade ending at the second floor. The palazzetto is currently the seat of the Venetian Heritage Foundation.

For fifteen years the foundation, which also has a New York office, has been supporting various cultural activities by organizing and funding restoration work, shows, publications, conferences, studies, and research projects, with the aim of preserving the huge heritage of Veneto art in Italy and in the territories that once were part of the Republic of Venice.

The most significant restoration work done includes the Chapel of the Ark of St. Anthony in Padua, the facades of the churches of the Gesuiti and of San Zaccaria in Venice, and the gilded silver altarpiece of the Church of San Salvador.

On the Dalmatian coast, Venetian Heritage has funded the restoration of the Orsini Chapel and Romanesque portal of the Cathedral of Traù (Trogir), in addition to the magnificent Gothic facade of St. Mark's Cathedral on Korčula.

CANNAREGIO

In olden times, vast canebrakes and swamps occupied the area of the Cannaregio quarter, called the *regio delle canne* (Canebrakes region), which explains the origin of the current name.

The city's second largest canal passes through the quarter: the Canal de Cannaregio, with its broad groundwork overlooked by some important palazzi, such as the Savorgnan and Manfrin residences, which had—and in part still have—vast gardens. Another such is Palazzo Labia, built by a wealthy family of Spanish descent and decorated by Tiepolo, who frescoed stories from the life of Mark Anthony and Cleopatra in the sumptuous ballroom and portrayed the lovely lady of the house, Maria Labia, as the queen of Egypt. The canal is spanned by two important bridges: the first, called Ponte delle Guglie because of the four obelisks that adorn it, goes back to the late sixteenth century; the second, a major architectural work by Andrea Tirali, takes its name from its three arches.

Not far from the latter stands Palazzo Surian-Bellotto, one-time residence of French ambassador Montaigue and his secretary, Jean-Jacques Rousseau. Just beyond once stood Palazzo dei Valier, famed for its frescoed facade and splendid garden, which even had a green theater.

The little-known Church of San Giobbe is a veritable trove of early Renaissance art. The Spanish embassy was in nearby Lista di Spagna.

The extant palazzo was rebuilt in the mid-eighteenth century by His Excellency the Count de Montealegre, who is buried in his chapel in the nearby Church of San Geremia. The Ghetto, with its towering houses—virtually Europe's first skyscrapers—and ancient synagogues still intact, testifies to the multiethnic political and cultural life of the Serenissima. The long Sensa, Madonna dell'Orto and Misericordia canals run parallel to one another along traces of preexistent agricultural cultivations of the Roman age. Overlooking their sunny and silent quays with southern exposure are some interesting minor palazzi and very important churches, such as the Church of the Madonna dell'Orto, where Tintoretto painted some of his best works. Also situated in this solitary locale is the Church of Sant'Alvise, where no less than three masterpieces by Gian Battista Tiepolo are kept. Taking busy Strada Nova parallel to the Grand Canal, one can spot the back of Palazzo Vendramin Calergi, where Richard Wagner finished *Parsifal*. He died there in 1883. Ca' d'Oro, Ca' Sagredo, and ancient Ca' da Mosto follow one another on the Grand Canal, which the Rio del Fontego dei Tedeschi, marking the boundary between Cannaregio and the *sestiere* of San Marco, flows into.

PALAZZO MANGILLI VALMARANA

The palazzo was built by will of Joseph Smith, Consul of His Majesty George III of England to the Republic of Venice. The new building rose where fourteenth-century buildings owned by the Soranzo once stood.

For years Joseph Smith, arrived from Great Britain to learn the art of commerce, rented the ancient residence, at the time occupied by the Williams, English bankers. A few years later he managed to buy the property, whereupon he assigned Antonio Visentini the job of erecting a new building imitative of classical style, as well as building his villa in Mogliano Veneto, today no longer extant. The consul was one of the leading collectors and art dealers of his time. He launched Canaletto on the English market and commissioned numerous views of Venice from the same painter. He was the friend and patron of Sebastiano and Marco Ricci. A large part of the famous collection was purchased by the Royal House of England.

In 1784, shortly after Smith's death, the palazzo was sold to Count Giuseppe Mangilli, a patron of the arts with a neoclassical penchant, who assigned the complete renovation of the building and the raising of two floors to architect Giannantonio Selva. The prevailing taste in Europe toward the end of the eighteenth century was Louis Seize. Comfort began to play a part in the new lifestyle; rooms were smaller and lighter and more rigorous symmetrical decorations were created.

Selva brought a wave of modernity to the lagoon, especially following his sojourns in Paris and England, where he came under the influence of Robert Adam, evident in the use of Wedgwood blue in certain stuccos used to decorate rooms.

Forward-thinking architect Selva probably designed every detail of the residence from the furnishings to the fireplaces and wall and ceiling decorations. Here, for the first time in Venice, a real bathroom was introduced, complete with a shapely sunken tub fashioned from a single block of Carrara marble. Frescoes by Pier Antonio Novelli and Gianbattista Canal decorate the rooms. The main floor has been magnificently restored by the Buziol Foundation.

The decorations of Palazzo Mangilli were done exquisitely in every
room, from the octagonal vestiaire to the monochrome frescoes of the
bathroom, with its splendid tub made from a block of Carrara marble,
and the master bedroom with neoclassical alcove.

CA' SAGREDO IN SANTA SOFIA

Certain elements of the facade of the palazzo built for the Morosini family on the Grand Canal denote its Veneto–Byzantine origin. The second floor windows, with round raised arches borne by polychrome marble columns, go back to this period. The upper main floor was added in the fourteenth century. To the new four-light window were added some older, sculpted, decorative friezes, probably salvaged during the enlargement of the old building. Present in Venice since the ninth century, the Sagredo became part of the Maggior Consiglio in 1100, after Venice regained control over the city of Sibenik in Dalmatia.

At the outset of the eighteenth century, Gherardo Sagredo bought the palazzo and undertook a vast project to renovate and enlarge the building under the supervision of Andrea Tirali, who designed a striking two-flight staircase with walls and ceilings painted in 1734 by Pietro Longhi. The frescoes depict the fall of the giants and are inspired by those executed by Giulio Romano two hundred years earlier for Palazzo Te in Mantua. The ambitious project began with the construction of the ballroom, double in height on the Strada Nova side, decorated with paintings by Gaspare Diziani, but it was never completed. Gherardo Sagredo, Procuratore of San Marco, wanting to finish the work, commissioned Temanza to produce a new plan for the facade on the Grand Canal. But when death took him, a lengthy dispute over the inheritance followed on into the late eighteenth century, when the city was no longer a capital but a province of the empire of Austria.

The interior was sumptuously decorated by the most famous stucco artists of the time, Abbondio Stazio and Carpoforo Mazzetti Tencalla from Ticino, responsible for the stuccowork of the grandest bedroom of Venice,

unhappily migrated to the United States at the turn of the twentieth century and currently at the Metropolitan Museum of New York. Luckily, the rooms of the Casino on the top floor have remained intact and constitute a stellar example of Venetian rococo stuccowork. During the recent restoration, the signatures of the two Ticino masters surfaced along with the date of execution of the stuccos: 1718. The volumes of the ornamentation and the original polychromes display a superb level of craftsmanship unequaled since this original and unusual decorative feat.

One of the rooms of the foyer is decorated with polychrome stuccos
depicting triumphant armigers.
On the ceiling, a series of exotic birds are represented in relief in pale-
blue sunken squares with molding. Above the doors, wild beasts come
out of the rich drapes falling from the cornices.

PALAZZO FONTANA SULLAM

In the mid-sixteenth century, the Fontana—native Piacenza merchants—relocated to Venice, where they made a fortune. At the turn of the seventeenth century, Giovanni Fontana had the palazzo, imitative of classical style, built on the Grand Canal and richly furnished with tapestries, precious Cordova leather items, and ceilings with decorated beams. At the end of the same century, part of the palazzo was rented to the Rezzonico family, who lived there for several years before moving into Palazzo Bon in San Barnaba, still unfinished at the time. In 1693, Carlo Rezzonico was born there and became pope in 1757 with the name Clement XIII.

With the fall of the republic, the Fontanas sold the palazzo to banker Reck; it later went to the Sullam family, who still owns it today. Some rooms are decorated with lavish eighteenth-century frescoes. Of great interest is the surpassingly rich library of Riccardo Calimani, famed writer and essayist, who set up a bookcase double the normal height in the central portego of the upper main floor.

CASA GUILLON MANGILLI BOVIO

In 1784, by will of new owner Count Giuseppe Mangilli, architect Giannatonio Selva added two floors to the palazzo built fifty years earlier by Consul Smith.

The rooms of this new section were decorated by the same artists who had worked on the main floor of the same palazzo.

The colors used for the stuccos and frescoes are typical of the second half of the eighteenth century, soft and elegant.

The entrance of the palazzo was originally preceded by an apse that acted as a screen between the garden and hall. An elegant neoclassical decoration is sculpted above the portal.

The owner, a descendant of the Mangilli, has furnished the apartment with furniture and other objects that have been in the palazzo for more than two hundred years. From the master bedroom one can admire the Ponte di Rialto and the old Erbaria markets. A contemporary light fixture designed by Massimo Micheluzzi has been installed in the dining room, which also features Venetian Louis Seize XVI chairs.

The motif of the frieze with the ox skull and laurel wreaths, sculpted on the lintel of the curved portal, is also found on the cornices of some rooms of the palazzo, as well as sculpted on the friezes of the consoles that furnish various rooms.

*Most of the furnishings of this residence were expressly created
for the purpose in the late eighteenth century. The ceiling is decorated
with* marmorino *stuccos and plasters, and with grotesques painted by
Giovanni Battista Canal.*

THE TREASURES
OF CANNAREGIO

CA' PRIULI VENIER MANFRIN

CA' D'ORO

SCUOLA VECCHIA DELLA MISERICORDIA

FARMACIA SANTA FOSCA

CHIESA DEGLI SCALZI

CHIESA DI SAN GIOBBE

CHIESA DEI GESUITI

SINAGOGA CANTON

SINAGOGA TEDESCA

CA' PRIULI VENIER MANFRIN

The Priuli of San Geremia came from a poor branch of a very old noble family, which toward the middle of the fifteenth century inherited some properties near Ponte delle Guglie.

In the following centuries, the family accumulated a fortune while continuing to invest in real estate, always in the same area. By the close of the seventeenth century, the Priuli of San Geremia were part of the narrow group of leading families who had the destiny of the republic in their hands. Giovanni Priuli went through all the stages of a political career necessary to become Procuratore of San Marco in 1723, thus crowning the centuries-old ambitions of the family. To celebrate the political success achieved, the family needed a real residence worthy of its rank, not one inferior to the ones built recently by the Savorgnans and by the Labias a short way from the old Priuli houses. In 1727 the Istrian stone facade was raised on the Canale di Cannaregio, based on a design by architect Andrea Tirali, to whom also goes the merit of having designed the elegant paving of St. Mark's Square. Tirali was surely inspired by Ca' Zenobio, built some thirty years previous by Antonio Gaspari, but eliminated the architectural orders from the facade. He had the entrance hall run along the facade, and consequently, the through salon on the lower main floor as well, providing the latter with a gallery to create a ballroom twice as high as the other rooms. Perhaps for the first time in Venice, a Roman-style inner courtyard broke with the classic layout of the Venetian palazzo, which in this case runs around the courtyard itself. Twenty years later Massari put forward the same architectural solution for the design of Palazzo Grassi.

The Venier inherited the palazzo in the latter half of the eighteenth century, and shortly thereafter, in 1787, sold it to Count Girolamo Manfrin, a wealthy and able businessman with a murky past, who obtained the tobacco franchise from the Republic. Manfrin commissioned painter Giambattista Mengardi and decorator Davide Rossi to completely redo every room in the vast palazzo with mythological allegories and refined stuccos, and gathered an important collection of rare books and more than four hundred paintings of the Veneto school, among which is the *Tempest* by Giorgione.

Preceding pages: Ballroom ceiling by Giambattista Mengardi and Davide Rossi, Phaeton Asks Apollo for the Chariot, *1787. Above: details of stuccos and frescoes in some* *rooms on the lower main floor of the palazzo.*

262

The rooms of this mansion, together with those of Palazzo Mangilli, are the city's most luxurious example of Louis Seize.

The little-known building exemplifies early eighteenth-century Veneto neoclassical architecture, which forerunner Tirali

introduced in the city. The palazzo is now owned by the Veneto Region.

CA' D'ORO
GIORGIO FRANCHETTI GALLERY

At the beginning of the fifteenth century, Marino Contarini, who belonged to one of the most illustrious families of the Serenissima, wed Soradamor Zeno, also a member of an old Venetian family, who brought a dowry of the Veneto-Byzantine palazzo built in the twelfth century.

Contarini purchased some adjoining properties and, in 1421, decided to rebuild and enlarge the old Zeno residence. In archive documents still in existence, the keen interest of the commissioning party in the new construction is mentioned, and the payroll lists the names of sculptor Matteo Raverti, already active in Milan in connection with the construction of the cathedral; of Giovanni and Bartolomeo Bon, Venetian architects and sculptors engaged in those years in the construction of the Porta della Carta of Palazzo Ducale; and of Giovanni di Francia, to whom was assigned the gilding of the facade. The name of the building therefore comes from the gilded sculpted elements of the facade at the time. The splendor of the residence lasted but a few years. After Contarini's death, the palazzo changed hands a number of times and slowly deteriorated. In 1845, John Ruskin painted the palazzo facade in a state of semi-neglect in his notebook of Venetian watercolors. In those years, young Russian Prince Alexander Trubetzkoi bought the building as a gift to a famous étoile, ballerina Maria Taglioni. Architect Meduna, in the employ of the prince and ballerina, made a series of heavy-handed changes in Gothic Revival style that met with harsh criticism from contemporaries. After the property further changed hands, Baron Giorgio Franchetti bought it in 1894 and committed himself to the arduous undertaking of restoring the building as it was in the fifteenth century. A refined collector and enlightened patron of the arts, Franchetti immediately thought of Ca' d'Oro as the right place for his collection, and thus turned the private residence into a museum and monument accessible to all, a decidedly modern concept in Italy at the turn of the century. In 1916 he signed a donation agreement with the national government whereby he undertook to cede the building in exchange for funding that would allow him to complete the restoration work. The works exhibited there include such masterpieces as the Saint Sebastian by Andrea Mantegna and the *Double Portrait* by Tullio Lombardo.

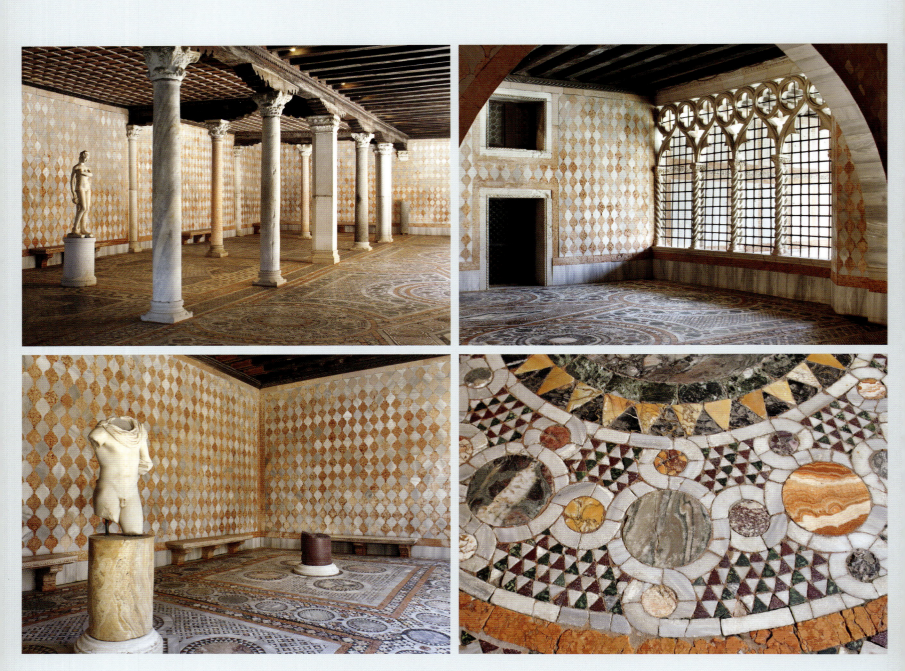

Baron Franchetti himself worked on the execution of the marble inlays of the floors. The models for the patterns of the flooring are after those of the Basilica of San Marco and the Basilica of San Donato in Murano. The choice of the individual marble was likewise under the direct supervision of Giorgio Franchetti. Some unused old elements are in the storerooms of the museum.

SCUOLA VECCHIA DELLA MISERICORDIA

The school stands in one of the city's rare solitary spots.

The old terracotta flooring of Campo dell'Abbazia, which dates from the fifteenth century (even if replaced several times), has a herringbone pattern framed by rectangular lengths of stone, and is the same as can be admired in the famous canvas by Gentile Bellini of the *Procession in St. Mark's Square* displayed at the Gallerie dell'Accademia.

The building, going back to the mid-fifteenth century, is probably the work of Giovanni and Bartolomeo Bon. The portal was surmounted by a monumental sculpted Istria stone lunette depicting Our Lady of Mercy, who was adored by the brothers, which found its way to London in the nineteenth century and is kept at the Victoria and Albert Museum.

At the beginning of the twentieth century, after years of neglect, painter and antique dealer Italico Brass restored the building and gathered his famed art collection there. Since 1983 the Scuola Vecchia has been housing the restoration workshops of the Gallerie dell'Accademia State Museum. The vast room on the second floor is where large paintings are restored. The building is surrounded by a pretty garden with tall cypresses and a magnificently preserved Gothic loggia.

FARMACIA SANTA FOSCA

Here we have the oldest pharmacy in Venice, still at its original location (some pharmacy rooms have been rebuilt and installed at the Museo del Settecento Veneziano of Ca' Rezzonico, a museum focused on eighteenth-century Venice).

The beamed ceilings are decorated in the style of Sansovino; most of the richly carved wooden furnishings date from the late seventeenth century. In recent times some busts situated between the broken curvilinear tympanums over the doors have been attributed to Francesco Pianta, the virtuoso sculptor of the boiseries of the Scuola Grande of San Rocco. As always in Venice, the wood left in sight is walnut. The prized veneers of the same wood were used to adorn the large geometric panels of the doors and boiseries. The counters, also walnut, exemplify eighteenth-century taste, as do the four lovely ornamental wooden jars placed in the windows, painted in imitation of red porphyry.

From the other side of the old windows on Strada Nova, one can admire this one-of-a-kind "museumized" place where time stopped three hundred years ago. Entrance is from the adjoining modern pharmacy, open for business.

CHIESA DEGLI SCALZI

Baldassarre Longhena was asked by the Order of Our Lady of Mount Carmel, which had been established in Venice in the mid-seventeenth century, to build a church where once there were just a kitchen and ornamental gardens.

The generosity of Count Girolamo Cavazza, whose coat of arms is visible in the middle of the pediment of the facade, meant cost was no object in carrying out the construction. As a result, today the Church degli Scalzi can be considered a paragon of baroque architecture in Venice. The Carrara marble front is the work of Giuseppe Sardi, Longhena's pupil. Inside one is struck by the rich polychromy of the marble and by the incredible magnificence. The walls of the nave are faced with "old African marble," while the high altar's lovely spiral columns bear a small temple designed by Longhena, over which cherubs and little angels fly about. The large candlesticks of blue Murano glass placed by one of the side altars are remarkable, as are the doors inlaid with mother-of-pearl, lapis lazuli, and semiprecious stones representing exotic birds and bunches of flowers. Unfortunately, in 1915 an Austrian bomb destroyed the grandiose fresco by Tiepolo that depicted the *Transport of the Holy House of Loreto*.

However, in two side chapels the frescoes that the great artist painted in 1724 remain. The last doge of Venice, Ludovico Manin, is buried in this church.

The Manin Chapel is adorned everywhere by polychrome marble. Projecting from the side windows are drapes complete with fringes, executed in Verde Antique and yellow Sienna marble. The doors are also inlaid with thin pieces of marble, while a pair of candlesticks, as well as the altar, are fashioned from French red and Carrara white marble. Two splendid deep-blue glass candlesticks, produced in Murano at the beginning of the eighteenth century, are mounted in a silver structure, unfortunately oxidized. The Venier Chapel is also faced with polychrome marbles. The ebonized doors, with marble and semiprecious stone inlays, are probably the work of skilled Florentine workers.

CHIESA DI SAN GIOBBE

In 1378, pious Giovanni Contarini had a hospice for poor people built next to his home. Daughter Lucia welcomed the Friars Minor there and dedicated the chapel belonging to it to Saint Job.

In the first years of the fifteenth century Franciscan Fra' Bernardino da Siena came to the hospice and preached for a long time in the city on the lagoon. He was proclaimed a saint in 1450, just six years after his death. Doge Cristoforo Moro, who had known the friar and had found him to be a fascinating figure, allocated considerable funds for the realization of a Gothic church where the little chapel once stood. The new church was named in honor of Saint Job and Saint Bernardino. During his rule Moro earmarked over 10,000 ducats for the improvement and embellishment of the church, which was still unfinished at his demise. In his will (1471) he specified that architects Antonio Gambello and Lorenzo di Gianfrancesco be assigned to continue the work, who, however, were replaced shortly thereafter by young Pietro Lombardo, whose ingeniousness Doge Moro probably had sensed prior to his death. Lombardo's first work, dated 1470, is the main portal with its wealth of Franciscan allegories: a thorn bush that as it rises turns little by little into vine shoots that intertwine with flowers, fruits, and a little bird perched on a branch with outstretched wings. The capitals are likewise adorned with spirals of vine tendrils that enwrap cascades of flowers. The church, consecrated in 1493, has a nave without side aisles, interesting owning to its asymmetry: on the left, five chapels follow in succession, while on the right, four altars stand side by side.

In accordance with his last will and testament, Doge Moro is buried barefoot in Franciscan habit beside his wife underneath the floor in front of the altar in the middle of the main chapel.

The chapel dedicated to Giovanni Martini, merchant of Lucca, is the work of Antonio Rossellino, while the polychrome bas-reliefs of the ceiling are a Della Robbian work.

The sixteenth-century wooden choir of the Franciscans is situated in back of the high altar. In this building the quality of the reliefs carved by Pietro Lombardo and sons reaches a peak. The vault of the Martini Chapel is decorated with glazed polychrome terracotta elements coming from Tuscany.

CHIESA DEI GESUITI

Founded in 1148 by Cleto Gussoni, the church belonging to the Order of Crociferi was surrounded by gardens, vineyards and swamps, and stood by a hospital founded for the care of impoverished patients.

In 1523, the religious complex was visited by Ignatius of Loyola, who later embarked in Venice on a pilgrimage to Jerusalem. Upon his return in 1535, with a group of companions with whom in the meantime he had founded the Society of Jesus, he was ordained priest in this church. Sold by the Serenissima to the Jesuits for 50,000 ducats, the church, deemed too inadequate for the new order, was razed and rebuilt in 1715 by architect Domenico Rossi, who had to adhere to rigid schemes in line with the "Jesuit style." The work was funded by the Manin family of Friuli, which, eager to show its munificence, paid no heed to expense for the decoration of the nave, the presbytery, and the high altar. The decorative effects are marvelous: the pulpit features drapes and a carpet of white Carrara and Thessaloniki green marble, the work of Giuseppe Pozzo, which, if seen at even a slight distance, seems covered with precious damask; flitting stucco *putti*, little angels and cherubs—executed by two great artists of the time, Abbondio Stazio and Carpoforo Mazzetti Tencalla, very active in eighteenth-century Venice—bear the baldacchino encrusted with lapis lazuli. The ceiling frescoed by Francesco Fontebasso is beautiful, in one portion of which Abraham is depicted adoring the three angels. In a side chapel there is an Assumption by a young Tintoretto, while in the sacristy we find very good paintings by Palma il Giovane. In the first chapel to the left we can now admire the *Martyrdom of St. Lawrence*, a grandiose painting that Titian painted late in life (1559), magnificently restored today.

The facade of the church is completely built of Istria stone. Numerous colossal statues decorate the niches and architraves.

The marble carpet of the high altar is covered with Verde Antique and yellow Sienna marble elements.

A two-color scheme formed by white Carrara and Verde Antique marble reigns inside the church. The motif of the eighteenth-century Venetian fabrics is repeated on the columns and walls of the chapels and nave. The marble hangings of the baldacchino of the pulpit, magnificently executed, take up the two-color scheme and the motifs of the building's decorations.

SINAGOGA CANTON

The name of this old temple almost certainly comes from the building's location at the corner—"*canton*" in Veneto dialect—of the Ghetto Novo canal. Founded in 1531, it was the first synagogue of Venice conceived with a layout with twofold focus: the *Bimà*, or pulpit, and the *Aròn*, the closet that contains the Sepher Torah, or scrolls of the law.

Redesigned several times over the centuries, the synagogue assumed its current baroque look with rococo accents at the beginning of the eighteenth century. The *Aròn* is the only surviving decorative element of the late sixteenth century. The wooden decoration represents a unicum in Europe, owing to the presence of gold panels depicting biblical episodes taken from the book of Exodus, and carved amid rocaille motifs in relief. Recognizable scenes include the Red Sea passage, the sacrificial altar, the descent of the manna, the gift of the Torah, and Moses making water spring from the rock. The pews and the first tier of boiseries are walnut, while the panels with scenes from the Bible, and the open ovals—which on one of the two long sides of the temple acted as gratings for the small section reserved for women—are completely golden. The *Bimà* is situated under a low rounded arch held up by four golden wood columns with open-work shafts in skillful imitation of vine shoots. The apse ceiling is decorated with white-and-green stuccos dating from the eighteenth century and by an octagonal cupola topped by eight small windows for light; it is the only architectural element of the synagogue visible from Campo del Ghetto Novo.

SINAGOGA TEDESCA

The German Synagogue, or Sinagoga Tedesca, which follows the Ashkenazi rites, is the oldest in the Ghetto of Venice. It was built in 1528 and altered in 1732. It was built with a central layout centered on the pulpit or *Bimà*. Toward the end of the eighteenth century, structural issues of stability began to appear, still evident on the Venetian-style floor.

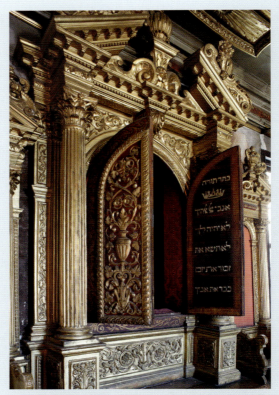

The heavy structure of the pulpit was later shifted from the middle for positioning between windows that overlook Campo del Ghetto Novo to reduce stress on the weak floor. Opposite the *Bimà* is the *Aròn Ha Qòddesh*, which, together with the main portal, are the only wooden decorations from the sixteenth-century synagogue; their style recalls the altars of the churches and the portals of the houses and palazzi of Venice at the close of the sixteenth century. The irregular plan of the German Synagogue is made harmonious by the inclusion of an elliptical *matroneo* for female worshippers and by the plastered walls frescoed to resemble marble. The height of the ceiling cannot fail to remind one of certain ballrooms in Veneto palazzi and villas built at the turn of the eighteenth century. The Museo Ebraico (Jewish Museum) was founded in 1954 and expanded by connecting some apartments by the three old synagogues—German, Canton, and Italian—which are part of the museum circuit. Some precious old Jewish liturgical objects are kept there, as well as rare books.

In 2016, on the occasion of the fifth centennial of the Ghetto of Venice, the Venetian Heritage Foundation, in collaboration with the Jewish Community of Venice, decided to launch an international fundraising campaign to completely reorganize the exhibition space of the museum and to restore the three old synagogues.

GIUDECCA

Giudecca is considered the biggest of the islands that form the city of Venice, although it actually comprises a whole of eight islets, linked by bridges.

In former times it was known as Spinalonga, to its elongated herringbone shape. The origin of its current name is uncertain, the most plausible explanation being that it comes from "*zudegà*," dialect for "*giudicato*," or "judged."

Tradition has it that during the ninth century, the Republic granted the lands of Spinalonga to compensate some families who were unjustly exiled. The north side of the island overlooks the Giudecca Canal; the important monuments there include the Church del Redentore, a masterpiece by Andrea Palladio, erected by will of the senate of the Republic following deliverance from the pestilence of 1576, while on the south side, sheltered from the winds and exposed to the sun, are found the famed gardens of Giudecca, many of which were planted as early as the sixteenth century around smaller villas, places of amusement and delight. In the torrid summertime, patricians would retreat there, fleeing Venice in search of cooler temperatures.

With the coming of the industrial era at the close of the nineteenth century, various factories and shipyards sprung up. With its impressive size, Molino Stucky stands witness to that moment in history. Shortly thereafter, the Birra Dreher brewery was built, next to which the Fortuny factory rose a few years later.

At the beginning of the twentieth century, there were still many truck gardens here, with produce being sold at the Rialto market. There was even a dairy farm.

For more than twenty years now, Giudecca has found a new identity, thanks to many enlightened foreigners who have decided to make it their home, among other things, to enjoy the best view of the city every day.

FORMER DREHER BREWERY

At the turn of the twentieth century, Giudecca underwent important changes due to the growing, albeit belated, industrialization of a country unified not long since.

Big industrial buildings were erected on the island, such as Molino Stucky, the Junghans factory, and various shipyards. The warehouses of the Dreher Brewery were among them.

After years of neglect, the warehouses were finally renovated in the 1980s for use as ateliers and as homes by painters, photographers, architects, and artists.

Laura Diaz de Santillana is a successful, internationally recognized Venetian artist.

A few years ago she decided to move to one of the lofts once used as a warehouse by the brewery. She has followed her father's footsteps: Ludovico Diaz de Santillana was artistic, and designer of the Venini kiln, while her maternal grandfather was Paolo Venini, founder of the famed Murano firm that still bears his name today.

Laura's artistic production could not but be tied to glass, even though she works with various materials, including marble, bronze, paper, and fabrics. The walls of her loft are lined with books, part of which belonged to the family, on light metal bookshelves devised by her father.

A monolithic piece of furniture that contains his glass objects and designs separates the studio from the large space, twice the normal height, practically furnished with nothing more than books and glass objects. *Big Flats* is the name of the latest blown-glass sculptures, shaped and compressed, created by Laura in Seattle with the help of a master American glassblower.

Above and opposite: Glass sculptures by Laura de Santillana from the collection Big Flats.
The thin metal bookcases were designed by Ludovico Diaz de Santillana.

The ample high-ceilinged space has been divided in part by a two-tier bookcase.

Other industrial structures converted into ateliers and homes can be seen from the semicircular window. The sculptures on the table are the work of the owner of the house.

LA CASA ROSSA AL REDENTORE

To the right of the white facade of the Church del Redentore, a plain two-story house of minor architecture—probably built at the end of the sixteenth century—marks the end of the square on one side, and on the other side, overlooks the Giudecca Canal. The building is covered with *coccio pesto* (crushed earthenware) plaster in the same tonality chosen by Palladio for the plaster that has been covering the sides of the majestic temple for five hundred years. The reddish house, in a sorry state when the current owners bought it a few years ago, has been turned into a cozy abode. The walls of some of the rooms are decorated with Cordova leather.

Every window in the house affords a spectacular view, which begins from the Island of San Giorgio and ends with Molino Stucky. To the rear of the house is a small garden with pergolas and creepers, dominated by the architectural elements of the church. At the bottom of the garden is an old warehouse in typical Venetian style, once used to store goods or salt, or as at the Arsenale, for rope production. Up until a few years ago, the building was used as a storeroom by a well-known Giudecca secondhand dealer. After scrupulous restoration work to preserve the original structures, the spacious sixteenth-century loft now has a swimming pool that rests on the ground like a huge piece of furniture, and guest rooms for the fortunate.

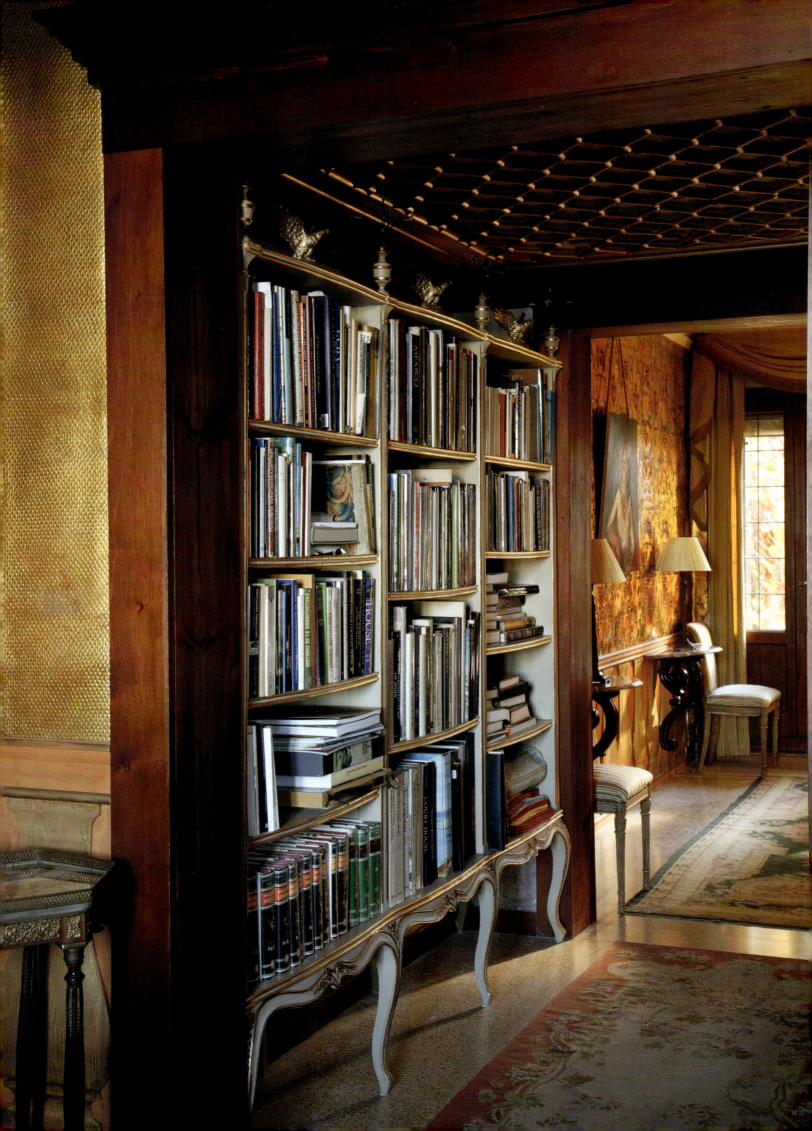

CASA BOMBASSEI AI TRE OCI

The top floor of the Gothic revival de Maria home, called the "Casa ai Tre Oci" because of the three large windows in front, has been the Venice residence of the Bombassei family of Bergamo since the late 1990s.

The apartment has been recently renovated by architect Luca Bombassei, who, rather than contend with the building, intelligently made the best of it.

The apartment's various terraces afford one of the most incredible views in the world. The Gothic Revival merlons of Istrian stone act as a balustrade to the central terrace, while the other terraces along the sides of the house are built of wood.

Most of the furnishings are contemporary, except for some eighteenth-century furniture.

THE FORTUNY FACTORY

Mariano Fortuny y Madrazo, born in Granada in 1871, followed in the footsteps of his parents: his father was a well-known painter from Catalonia, while his mother came from a family of artists and intellectuals. In 1889 the family settled in Venice, where young Fortuny began to take inspiration from the Asian world. In 1899 he took part in the Biennale and that same year married Henriette Nigrin. He became keen on photography and developed a consummate ability in the use of a new discovery—electric energy—and dealing with the problems of stage lighting, an art that he had begun to specialize in. In 1906, at Palazzo Pesaro degli Orfei, together with his wife, Henriette, he created the first workshop for the printing of textiles, mainly silks and velvets. In 1919, with World War I over, with great effort he resumed the textile business and, in partnership with Giancarlo Stucky, opened a new mill at Giudecca, founding the Società Anonima Fortuny. He enlarged an old pitch factory to install machinery of his own devising, for the printing and decoration of his cotton prints, employing techniques invented by him that became known worldwide. A few years after his death in Venice, the Fortuny widow donated Palazzo Pesaro and the collections kept there to the city. In 1949 the Fortuny factory became the property of an energetic American interior decorator, Elsie McNeill Lee. Known as "la Contessa" after wedding Alvise Gozzi, she devoted her life to promoting the renowned production and to keeping the artisanal secrets of the printing of textiles, still jealously guarded today. At present, brothers Maury and Mickey Riad run the house with unchanged enthusiasm; a short time ago they renewed the showroom of the historic Giudecca headquarters.

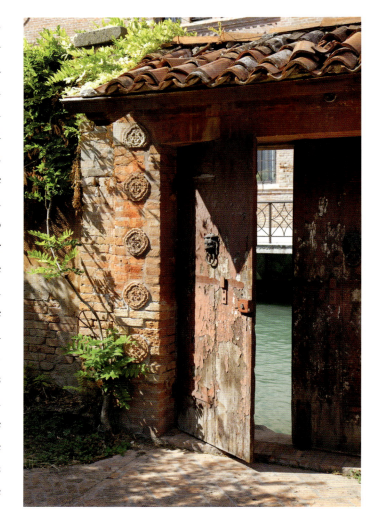

Big industry came to the lagoon at the beginning of the twentieth century. Giudecca was partially transformed to make room for the new industrial buildings.

FORMER CONVENT DELLE ZITELLE
GARDEN OF HOTEL BAUER PALLADIO

During the latter half of the sixteenth century, Jesuit preacher Benedetto Palmi took note of many poor orphan girls exposed to the temptations of the world. The Serenissima did not interfere with prostitution, which is why the pious priest founded a home for marriageable girls too poor to possess a dowry, hence the name *zitelle* (spinsters).

The construction of the church and convent complex got underway in 1582, on a model attributed to Palladio, and was completed after 1586 by builder Jacopo Bozzetto. A few years ago the former Renaissance convent was converted into a hotel. A vast garden was designed in back, which is divided into four distinct interconnected gardens. In the first, some magnificent trees, among which an old Aleppo pine and *Olea europaea* dominate the space in the middle of beds of roses, irises, columbines, and others. The large chestnut pergola covered with vines was designed by architect Giuseppe Rallo, who was brilliantly inspired by the gardens and wooden structures depicted by de' Barbari in his celebrated view of Venice, printed in 1500. As at that time, long vine bowers divide the gardens and are bordered by beds of irises and aromatic plants. In springtime hundreds of tulip and crocus bulbs bloom on the large meadow. The second garden is characterized by boxwood hedges flanked by large white hydrangeas, roses, and agapanthus in geometric flowerbeds around the trees. In the third garden, an age-old magnolia and big lime tree tower over hydrangeas and oleanders in bloom. The fourth garden is characterized by a camphor path. Here, too, narcissus and tulips alternate during the seasons with white and blue asters. Roses, clematis, and hydrangeas separate this garden from the others. Tomato plants, artichokes, and other vegetables typical of lagoon cultivations alternate with flowering shrubs, just as with the *hortus conclusus* of the oldest gardens. The credit for this wonderful green space goes to hotel owner Francesca Bortolotto Possati and her enthusiasm, and to the experience of architect Giuseppe Rallo, who has been looking after the park of Villa Pisani in Strà for years.

*Thanks to recent restoration work, the silent gardens of the
former Convento delle Zitelle have regained the sixteenth-century
appearance etched by de' Barbari in his famous map of the city
of Venice.*

CASA DEI TRE OCI
FONDAZIONE DI VENEZIA

The eclectic Casa dei Tre Oci was designed by artist Mario de Maria (Marius Pictor) in 1913, who was inspired by certain elements of Palazzo Ducale, such as the merlons and the three large windows. The result is one of Venice's most interesting examples of Gothic Revival architecture.

Built as a combination home and atelier at a time in history when Giudecca was an island marked by town planning and social transformation, de Maria personally supervised the construction work on his architectural whim.

The abode became the property of de Maria's son, Astolfo, also a painter, and his wife, Adele, who continued to make it a meeting place of intellectuals and artists. Fontana, Morandi, Hundertwasser, and many others were frequent guests.

In 2000, the property was purchased by the Fondazione di Venezia, which, after careful restoration recently completed, decided to use the former residence for exhibitions, with a focus on photography, a choice that has proved to be a great success.

The facade of the de Maria home borrowed certain elements typical of Venetian Gothic, such as the windows, merlons, and decorations on the exterior of Palazzo Ducale.

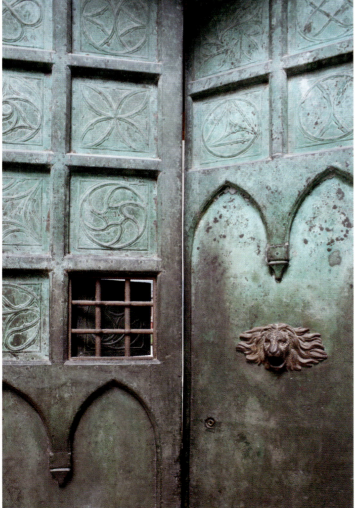

The main floor of the old de Maria home—called "dei Tre Oci"—is now used for photo exhibits. The furnishings, of different periods and styles, were collected by de Maria in the early twentieth century. They have been bound to the building.

Idea Books and the author thank:

James Ivory, Diane von Furstenberg, and Peter Marino

Archivio di Stato di Venezia, Comune di Venezia, Comunità Ebraica di Venezia, Conservatorio di Musica Benedetto Marcello, Fondazione Bru Zane, Fondazione Claudio Buziol, Fondazione Giorgio Cini, Fondazione Musei Civici di Venezia, Fondazione Francois Pinault, Fondazione Venetian Heritage, Fondazione di Venezia, Frati Francescani minori di San Francesco della Vigna, Istituto Veneto di Scienze Lettere e Arti, IRE Istituto di Ricovero e di Educazione Venezia, Le Stanze del Vetro, Ministero dei Beni e delle Attività Culturali e del Turismo, Museo Storico Navale, Padri Gesuiti di S. Maria Assunta, Procuratoria della Basilica di San Marco, Regione del Veneto, Scuola Grande dei Carmini, Scuola Grande di San Rocco, Soprintendenza per i Beni Architettonici e Paesaggistici of the provinces of Venezia, Belluno, Padova and Treviso, Soprintendenza speciale per il patrimonio storico artistico ed etnoantropologico e per il polo museale of the city of Venice and of the municipalities of Gronda lagunare, Ufficio Beni Culturali della Curia di Venezia.

Fabio Achilli, Giancarlo Adorno, Aman Canal Grande Hotel, Marcella Ansaldi, Giberto and Bianca Arrivabene Valenti Gonzaga, Anna Barnabò, Luigi Bassetto, Shaul Bassi, Hotel Bauer, Gloria Beggiato, Gabriella Belli, Maria Novella Benzoni, Martin Bethenod, Luigi and Gesy Bisiach, Elisabetta Boetti Falck, Luca Bombassei, the Bon family, Elisabetta Borgazzi Barbò Rubin de Cervin Albrizzi, Francesca Bortolotto Possati, Letizia Bovio Guillon Mangilli, Cristiana Brandolini d'Adda, Giancarlo and Giorgia Bussei Canone, Riccardo and Anna Vera Calimani, Carla Calisi, Giovanni Caniato, Hotel Ca' Sagredo, Giorgio Ceccato, Agnese Chiari Moretto Wiel, Alvise and Andrea Chiari Gaggia, Claudia Cremonini, Paolo and Aud Cuniberti, Giovanna Damiani, Roberto De Feo, Jean Marie and Gaby Degueldre, Laura Diaz de Santillana, Cecilia Falck Collalto, Farmacia Santa Fosca, Fortuny, Ferigo and Claudia Foscari Widmann Rezzonico, Tonci and Barbara Foscari Widmann Rezzonico, Martina Frank, Silvio Fuso, Pasquale Gagliardi, Paolo Gnignati, Isabelle Jourdain Patti, David Landau and Marie-Rose Kahane, Gaetano and Barbara Maccaferri, Giulio Manieri Elia, Valentina Marini Clarelli Nasi, Mons. Antonio Meneguolo, Hotel Metropole, Giorgio and Ilaria Miani, Romilly McAlpine, Pier Luigi Pizzi, Giuseppe Rallo, Maury and Mickey Riad, Olivia Richli, Lidia Salmon Fasoli, Ignacio and Gola de Segorbe, Chiara Squarcina, Diego Vecchiato, Guido Venturini, Costanza Verga Paladini.

Photo credits
For all photos in this book: © Jean-François Jaussaud, with the exception of the photos on pp. 9, 10, 11, and 12: © James Ivory

Illustrations
Ludovico Ughi, *Iconografica rappresentatione della Inclita Citta di Venezia consacrata al Reggio Serenissimo Dominio Veneto*, 1729, Archive photograph - Fondazione Musei Civici di Venezia
p. 5: Iron prow piece in the shape of ducal horn, eighteenth century, Venice, Italy, Metropolitan Museum of Art
p. 11: Vittore Carpaccio, *Miracolo della reliquia della Croce al ponte di Rialto*, Venezia, Gallerie dell'Accademia, Soprintendenza Speciale PSAE e polo museale veneziano – Archive photograph
p. 12: Vittore Carpaccio, *Incontro e partenza dei fidanzati*, Venezia, Gallerie dell'Accademia, Soprintendenza Speciale PSAE e polo museale veneziano – Archive photograph
p. 13: Giorgione, *La tempesta*, Venezia, Gallerie dell'Accademia, Soprintendenza Speciale PSAE e polo museale veneziano – Archive photograph

Graphics
Marco de Sensi

Editorial project
Graziella Pasquinucci

First published in the United States of America in 2016 by
Rizzoli International Publications, Inc.
300 Park Avenue South - New York, NY 10010
www.rizzoliusa.com

Originally published in Italian in 2015 by
Idea Books
Via Regia 53 - 55049 Viareggio - Italy
www.ideabooks.com

© 2015 IdeArte srl

Third Printing, 2017
2017 2018 2019 2020 / 10 9 8 7 6 5 4 3

ISBN: 978-0-8478-4816-4

Library of Congress Control Number: 2015944951

Printed in Italy